The Art and Science
of Communication

The Art and Science of Communication

Tools for Effective Communication in the Workplace

P.S. Perkins

WILEY

John Wiley & Sons, Inc.

Illustrator Emilio Lee.

Published by John Wiley & Sons, Inc., Hoboken, New Jersey.
Published simultaneously in Canada.

For general information on our other products and services or for technical support, please contact our Customer Care Department within the United States at (800) 762-2974, outside the United States at (317) 572-3993 or fax (317) 572-4002.

Wiley also publishes its books in a variety of electronic formats. Some content that appears in print may not be available in electronic books. For more information about Wiley products, visit our web site at www.wiley.com.

Library of Congress Cataloging-in-Publication Data:

Perkins, P.S., 1959–
   The art and science of communication : tools for effective communication in the workplace / P.S. Perkins.
      p.   cm.
   "Published simultaneously in Canada."
   Includes index.
   ISBN 978-0-470-24759-4 (cloth: alk. paper)
   1. Business communication. 2. Interpersonal communication. 3. Persuasion (Rhetoric) I. Title.
   HF5718.P475   2008
   651.7—dc22

                                         2008001378

Printed in the United States of America.

10 9 8 7 6 5 4 3 2 1

Dedicated to NJ, who gave me
the grace and courage to stand alone,
but made the choice to stand beside me
to speak and live truth in the WORD.

Contents

CONTENTS

Contents

CONTENTS

Foreword

Les Brown

I firmly believe you have to accept yourself before others can accept you. The fact that myself and so many others have come to know, appreciate, and respect Pamela Perkins says a lot about her self-acceptance. And why wouldn't she esteem such confidence and self-assurance? With such an impressive background of intrapersonal, interpersonal, nonverbal, and intercultural communication practices—spanning a 20-year period—she is certainly a living example of the greatness she teaches others to achieve.

Pamela's belief that "the universe is an equal opportunity employer, giving us all the exact same vocation—to create our lives" is my sentiment as well. But even though we all contain that same breath of creative energy, each and every one of us is infused with our own unique gift. After watching the creative energy of Pamela on the set of the motivational film, *Pass It On*—in which we were both featured—I must conclude that she is truly operating within her gift.

Any person who is determined to take control of his or her professional and personal success will greatly benefit from the teachings in *The Art and Science of Communication: Tools for Effective Communication in the Workplace*. One revelation featured in the book, Pamela's *Communication Staircase*®, will surely awaken you to your ability to effectively use communication as your primary tool of purposeful action! Workplace communication

---

Les Brown is a world-renowned motivational speaker. As a best-selling author, his books include *Live Your Dreams*, *It's Not Over Until You Win*, and *Up Thoughts for Down Times*. Visit www.lesbrown.com.

is one of the most difficult abilities to master, yet Pamela offers you the formula for success! It's truly an art *and* a science!

So what are you waiting for? Dive right in, devour these pages thoroughly and thoughtfully, and take control of the daily communication experiences that affect your relationships, career, and family, as well as every aspect of your personal, social, and professional well-being!

Acknowledgments

My deepest gratitude to:

Betty Perkins Jones, my mother, my *hero,* my friend and my father, **Palmer L. Perkins, Jr.,** who *always* found a way and consistently shared the blessed assurance that I had the strength to follow my heart;

Bernell Jones, a true educator, still doing the shot-gun and out dancing us all in the dance of life;

Lisa Hagan, my agent, and our friend **Jim Jermanok,** who both believed in the power of communication to change lives and my ability to be the channel;

To my loving siblings, **Beverly, Natalie, Jackie, Palmer, Tony,** and **Stephanie,** who still believe in dreams coming true;

Tresa, Sheri, and **Cathy,** whose support kept us afloat when the ship took on water;

Shad and Iain, true friends closer than a brother;

M&Y, R&J, M&C, A&RK, K&S, the family who came to the rescue and stayed;

Edward T. Hall, cultural anthropologist, who encouraged me to help "free my people";

The Speech Communication departments that nurtured me along the way including **Molly V.** and **Hope S.,** whose spirits keep the dream alive;

Mother Billie Marrs, who never abandoned her love or faith in me;

Big brother **Nathan** and big sister **Peyton,** whose zest for life gives me hope;

ACKNOWLEDGMENTS

Tim and **Tadhi** and the determination to *Stand-in-Truth;*

The ***Pass It On* family** for welcoming me into the movement to keep Passing It On;

ByteAll Media Inc., joining me for the next phase of this incredible adventure;

Mama Clara and the spirit of all my ancestors who believed in the power of the word to free their minds, bodies, and spirits;

And foremost, to the Christ within that gives me the strength and courage to serve and be the change I want to see.

For many years, I shielded and guarded my gift and understanding of the power of words behind the safety of academic walls. Semester after semester, I was challenged to come out of hiding to build the entity that became the inspiration for the completion of this book, the Human Communication Institute. Adults and youth consistently asked why they were never taught the important nature and tools of communicating and listening and felt if they had, their marriages, careers, children, and communities would be so much better off. Groups, organizations, and businesses came forward to inquire and understand the art and science of communication as the primary tool of organizational effectiveness. What you are about to read is the understanding, wisdom, art, and science of hundreds of teachers, theorists, students, and colleagues who shared, nurtured, and challenged my understanding of this powerful human gift. Their teachings have become my life. I pray that I have represented them well and I give credit where credit is due—the gift of the WORD, our power of creation, and the major tool to a better career, a better life, a better world.

Finally, I acknowledge the readers who have the courage to join me on this journey and use the power of the Communication Staircase Model to create the life they were born to live!

Introduction

It's time for a conversation, a *conversation about communication*. This is your new and personal guide to communication success in the workplace. You are about to have a different experience regarding words and their impact on you in the workplace and in your life. This conversation offers instructional support and encouragement as it introduces the daily communication processes we experience in organizational settings and show their interrelationship to one another. The *Communication Staircase Model* is the key to understanding your ability to take decisive and deliberate action. When we use communication as our primary tool of purposeful action, we can accomplish our personal and professional goals.

Through our words, we are individually creating our personal movie called *LIFE*. Communication is the common denominator of self-empowerment that every human being shares, regardless of race, class, gender, socioeconomic level, or environmental circumstances. There are few things in life we can say everyone (barring physiological circumstances) is equally endowed with, but the universal gift of thought and communication is one of them—the endowment of human reasoning and language. It is an amazing ability, one we take for granted but still the most powerful resource we have.

 Communication is synonymous with creation for humans.

Do you recognize the remarkable way words connect and disconnect us, especially in the business setting? Communication is the foundation of *all* behavior. ASC is a guide to help you understand the conscious connection between your communication and productivity. We communicate with one another by way of behavior. In defining communication, we should understand that *communication is experienced whenever meaning is attributed to current or past behavior.* Read this again carefully and understand the connection between how people relate to you and your behavior. Too often we think of communication as just words. Communication happens intentionally or unintentionally. Much of the "unintentional" communication transpires under the guise of nonverbal communication. However, we must learn that all effective communication happens only when intentional and that it is a behavioral *science!* Sociology, psychology, and cultural anthropology all have as their foundation the manner in which humans interact with themselves, one another, and their environments. Communication as a behavioral science transpires in a variety of arenas throughout our daily work experience. This guide is designed to bring these experiences together in a manner that clearly crystallizes and connects each occurrence. Each step builds upon another, empowering one another. We can no longer afford to leave the daily events of our lives, the workplace, or the planet, to continuously flowing verbal garbage. Millions are leading this life, a life where thoughts and words carelessly broadcasted create personal, professional, and collective chaos and misery.

We must realize the need to be responsible for the *words* that create our lives and ripple out to touch others. Human communication is socialization, the primary tool of enculturation. It is the framework under which we experience one another and the *reality* in which we individually and collectively live. This framework takes shape in the day-to-day contact we have with each other in our various daily communication activities, such as participating in the workplace.

THE COMMUNICATION STAIRCASE

Visualize a staircase that you must ascend several times a day. When you climb the staircase, you take one step at a time. When you try to double up or even triple up because you are in a hurry, you run the risk of slipping, tripping, or even falling. This is the way communication works. You are not effective on (or within) the third, fifth, or seventh step (or setting) if you don't take *one step at a time with the awareness AND skill necessary for that step!* Each step is crucial to the next. Each step has its own plateau, offers its own set of rules as well as its own challenges and potential for success. You build upon one step at a time to get to the top.

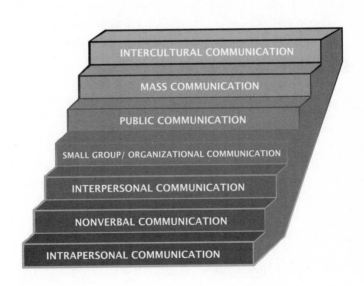

Did you notice from the diagram that each step exists during the course of your professional day, without exception? You awake and start your day with Intrapersonal messages setting the tone for the rest of your day. This step offers insight and tools into you as a communicator and the manner in which behavioral communication impacts your daily success. You take you wherever you go! The Nonverbal step helps you assess how you communicate with others using behavior that people see and feel more than they hear. Your Interpersonal Communication skills will soar with knowledge of the seven basic ingredients and the keys to effective listening. Your Small-Group experiences define your productivity at work by your ability to speak comfortably and competently with and in front of your coworkers. Public Presentation becomes a tool of advancement once you find your voice. Our awareness of the power and manipulation of Persuasive messages makes us better informed consumers and employees. Acquiring the skills that each preceding step offers allows any individual the capability to engage in Intercultural Communication comfortably and effectively with others in the organization with different perspectives. Each step builds upon the other, providing step-specific tools that enhance each communication arena. These are the same communication arenas you experience in your personal life *and* the same tools that will create personal success and happiness.

IN THE BEGINNING IS YOUR WORD . . .

Communication is an *inside-out* process whose effects expand like a ripple in a pool of water. We are all familiar with the shortcuts in life and those who take them. Where do most of those people end up? Back at the bottom step, even if they enjoyed a modicum of success at the top. Staying power comes from mastering the right steps, generally in the right order. Communication is rule governed, and the usage and creative manipulation of these rules largely depends on the type of communication and the setting in which it takes place. *The Art and Science of Communication: Tools for Effective Communication in the Workplace* will introduce the Communication Staircase, the tools and skills needed to create positive change in your professional career! It's time to take control of the daily communication experiences that affect your relationships, career, family, and every aspect of your personal, social, and professional well-being.

The greatest tool we all possess is the ability to think and speak the positive outcomes we want to see in life. Our words are the brushes we use to create life.

Why do most people think the way they do?

Because of the examples around them that become their storehouse of knowledge.

Are most people responsible for what they think?

Not when they are only spouting other people's stuff.

Most people are unaware that what they are speaking is just a replay of something they have been taught to think, right or wrong, healthy or unhealthy.

Why do most people appear to be living an unfulfilling life?

Most people perpetuate the same communication cycles they have been taught and thus keep re-creating other people's lives.

INTRODUCTION

We spend our entire waking and sleeping existence engaged in some form of communication. During the process of communication, we are informing, persuading, or entertaining. We go back and forth between these three forms of expression all day long in the workplace. Many don't realize that they primarily engage in only two forms of communication: informing and persuading. These forums of communication are rule governed. We witness these rules being applied in theories of management, marketing strategies, formal communications, and business networking. Depending on a complex set of preexisting rules of governance, we may or may not be successful each and every time. For most it's like playing the lottery: sometimes you win, but mostly you lose. Despite the fact that communication is rule governed, its successful application is completely personal. Understand, before you begin the thought that manifests into the word, the rules governing the listener, the setting, and other communication components are already present and working in the organizational environment. You bring your perspective to the mix and it becomes your *movie* creation. With this conversation, we are going to discuss your personal movie about *work.* Let's talk about a friend of mine, someone I'll call Jill. Her story offers a lens to observe the various settings interacting with one another as she calls them to life throughout her day.

Jill's day shares with us an employee's delicate balancing act of thoughts, words, and performance as she navigates the communication climate on her job. Her experiences climbing the Communication Staircase can offer insight into how easy it is to create and materialize the effects of our thoughts and words. Observe the beginning and progression of her day observing a few exchanges she has with herself and others.

Situation #1: Jill's First Thoughts in the Morning

Beep! Beep! Beep! What? What? Oh no! Get up! Damn, I can't be late today. I wish I had gone to the cleaners yesterday! Now what am I going to wear? TWENTY MINUTES!!!

And so starts Jill's day, or *your* day. It's a day that starts too often on the wrong foot. This is what the proverbial statement "getting up on the wrong side of the bed" means. Do these thoughts, words impact Jill's day? As her early morning continues . . .

Situation #2: Workplace Parking Lot

I hope I don't run into Richard this morning. I can't take his patronizing tone. It's as if all women are beneath him. He always shakes my hand like a wet fish! And every time he comes near me, that cologne! Yuck! I'm just gonna ignore him. Why does the division planning meeting have to be today of all days? I hate speaking in front of this group!

Notice the spiral of attraction. This attitude/energy/attraction followed her to the workplace. Now she is projecting through her thoughts and words how she feels.

Situation #3: Going into the Afternoon Division Meeting

I wish I had worn something else today. This blouse is too tight. Why didn't I go to the cleaners? I know they are going to all notice it when I speak this afternoon. God, why is everything so complicated? Man, I wish people would pull their weight. "Listen guys, we have got to get this together. Let's make a decision. No need to discuss who did what now!"

As we become convinced of our own lack of importance, competence, or worth, it becomes harder to communicate with others we might unknowingly put on a pedestal above ourselves. It becomes difficult to respond to spur-of-the-moment opportunities for self-expression.

Situation #4: Company Lunchroom

Oh, there she is again, Emiko. She is so together. She always has so much to contribute in the meetings. I should go over and introduce myself. Nah, I don't want to disturb her lunch. She probably wants to chill. I am sure she is tired of Americans always invading her space with "what is your background" questions.

Jill's cross-cultural experiences are jaded by her own inner conflict and lack of self-confidence.

Situation #5: Talking with Team Member at Meeting

"Oh, hey, David. Yeah, good to see you too. Things are going great! Uh, well, uh, OK, see you at the meeting." Oh my God! *What's wrong with me? Why didn't I say something? There was my chance!*

Jill is a prime example of how many of us just can't seem to find the right words at the right time.

Situation #6: At Jill's Desk

I can't believe this is happening! Stephanie being replaced? A new tracking system?! Why didn't I know about this? They can't just do this. There is nothing wrong with the old system. They are not going to get me to buy into this one! Why are they always trying to act busy fixing things that aren't broken?

Depending on the attitude of your target audience at any moment, the receptivity to your message is going to be affected.

Situation #7: The End of Another Work Day

This day can't be over soon enough. I'm so tired of this!
Jill's day ends as it began, full of frustration.

JILL'S PROFESSIONAL DESTINY?

There is a self-defeating energy striving to rule your day by distracting you from asking the right questions, thinking the right thoughts, and speaking the right words. What do I mean by "right"? That which is done with positive intention. The enemy? The nemesis in the greatest battle ever waged against humankind? Do you know the villain? The casualties of this war are far greater than ALL wars ever waged rolled up in one! That's right, the destruction of untold millions. Who is the enemy? Our own thoughts and words!

By our words we create "strange new worlds and boldly go where no man has gone before," as our friends on *Star Trek* remind us. By our words we create heaven and hell right here on earth. Critical thinking is *the finding, interpreting, integrating, and evaluation of information.* You are being invited to share in the critical thinking processes that will empower your professional life with the greatest tool you have—communication! Believe it! To truly realize the incredible significance of "In the beginning was the Word" you have to understand that it is YOUR WORD you are beginning with, *every moment of every day!* After absorbing and applying the skills in this guide, Jill and millions like her—people looking to make their professional lives into an experience worth living—will come to understand that, even if it doesn't solve everything, communication IS everything. We can experience healthy, productive, satisfying workplace environments. Take control and let's start with you.

Let the Conversation Begin!

The Art and Science
of Communication

Intrapersonal Communication

You Take *You* Wherever *You* Go

—P.S. Perkins

Give me a chance, Mr. Markham. I know I can lead the team. I ran this office for five years! Can't you see through Jim? What's wrong with you? It's my turn. You can't give it to him! It's my promotion. Mine! Mine!"

Beep! Beep! Beep!

Now you're awake and it was just a bad dream. Or was it? You're about to start your day and you had a fretful night. You're about to place your feet solidly back into the world. But wait. Before you do, are you sure you're awake? Yes, I know your eyes are open and you feel your heart beating. You're breathing, and you can probably feel the blood coursing through your veins if you're quiet enough. But are you awake? What about that dream? What a way to start the very day you're looking forward to your promotion. Let me give you a suggestion for getting back on the right track: Eat first, and then get out of bed. Yes, you read me right: eat first. We all understand breakfast is the most important meal of the day. We understand that we are what we eat. Many people are dedicated to starting their workday with the right kind of physical fuel to take them where they want to go. But what about their mental fuel? In the waking hours, just before you begin your workday, what kind of mental fuel do you feed yourself? It matters because this nourishment prepares you to handle the *mental* challenges of your day—personally, socially, and professionally.

"You are what you think" is the awareness and practice of the role *thoughts* fulfill in the moment-to-moment experiences of your life. Those moments begin over and over, begin with each waking breath as you move deliberately into consciousness. Your thoughts are the seeds that germinate the actions you will perform throughout your workday. What actions are you ready to perform today? It all depends on what thoughts you begin with every morning. Remember the expression "getting up on the wrong side of the bed"? We understand that this does not refer to a literal side of your physical bed! It is a metaphor for beginning your day with negative thoughts. And it's really true. If you wake up with negative thoughts and don't replace them immediately, you tend to carry those same negative thoughts and feelings around with you all day long. Ponder this—when have you had a bad start and been able to totally set it aside and perform your work duties without any mental or physical distractions? Chances are you took those same thoughts and emotions with you to the office and faked and/or fought your way through the day. You take *you* with you. You walked that attitude right into the office!

SELF-SABOTAGE OR SELF-FULFILLMENT?

The first step in achieving success in professional pursuits is mental preparation! We positively create our lives or we sabotage our lives. Most of us have associated sabotage with the act of undermining or backstabbing someone else. Truth sets you free—most individuals do more to undermine themselves than the combined efforts of everyone around them. The true sabotage lies within communication with oneself, in thoughts and words.

No one can think or speak to create your life for you!

Just as no one takes your place at work physically, no one can go to work for you mentally. That would be like asking a friend to eat your dinner and expecting you will be the one satisfied! The key is to arrive to work in a mental state you can positively thrive in. How can you use your thoughts to create the work environment you desire to prosper in?

DISCIPLINE OF THE MIND

The French philosopher Descartes was quoted as saying, "Except our own thoughts, there is nothing absolutely in our power." It is this power of thought that introduces the first step of the Communication Staircase. Intrapersonal Communication is the *communication you have with yourself about yourself and others*. It shares the inner workings of your mind with yourself. How often would you say you engage in mental chatter during the day? You talk to yourself more than you talk to anyone else. The important point is *how* you talk to yourself— what you say to yourself verbally and nonverbally.

Sizing up your internal communication is the first step, the basis of all other communication experiences within your work environment. It requires a lot of critical thought and awareness. When an individual pays serious attention to the daily conversations he has with himself, and critically examines the quality of experiences springing forth from these self-talks, he will be able to control more positively the materialization of the experiences around him. I use this word "materialization" literally. With our words we materialize the actions and events of our daily lives. You are either your greatest ally or your greatest adversary. We are all given the same empty screen as we start the *movie* of life. Then that screen fills with images and messages from our internal selves materializing into our external surroundings, including work. This ability to create our own movie, our own lives, is the gift and power shared by all humans.

 The universe is an equal opportunity employer giving each human the same vocation—to create their lives!

Our thoughts and words are the tools of creation, our pens and brushes. The process of creation is based on the same pattern of materialization shared by all species of creation. Specific conditions encourage creation. Seed + nutrient = tree. It is the same as Thought + word = action (or results). We create our lives with the brushstrokes of our thoughts and words! The *Human Communication Cocreation Theory* proposes that *Conscious thoughts + words + feelings → subconscious = materialization of life*. The purpose of the subconscious is to accept something as true, then create it. That's why feelings play an important role. They generally do not lie. This knowledge is important to experiencing the type of work environment you are thriving in. The environment starts within you. Many of us can immediately identify our work environments as either positive or negative. But do you realize those labels come from inside you? Too often we look at either of these realms as being simply the result of someone else's actions or responsibility— our bosses, employees, coworkers, management. Not true. Your life starts and ends with you. Do others play a role in the environmental attitude? Of course they do, but only to the extent that you allow them. And yes, sometimes the organizational environment can be so toxic that the decision before you is whether to stay and tough it out or walk away and create a new situation. But before you throw in the towel, take a look at what you are adding to the communication environment of the organization.

DIVE INTO YOUR LIFE!

Think of your life as a lake, a body of confined water. That which holds the lake in place—its banks, sediment, rocks, plants—represents your physical being, the body. The water in the lake represents your mind, your thoughts, the essence of your intellect or spirit that has no boundaries. Somehow the water, the internal you, continues to add to itself without ever overflowing its boundaries.

If I or someone else decided to fish in your lake on any given day at any given moment, what would we catch? Casting a rod into the depths of your mind would pull up what type of thoughts? When you go *fishing* into your own thoughts, second by second, what do you dredge up? How do you see yourself? What value do you place on yourself in comparison to others? Do you appreciate your coworkers? Do you respect your boss? Are you experiencing professional fulfillment at work?

Inside your *lake* are all the experiences and memories of your life. It is where you hold your values, attitudes, and beliefs. It is what houses that first birthday you remember, or your first kiss. It is that day at the park, or that first job and first promotion. It is also where you store the first harsh words you heard, the job you lost, emotional and physical abuse you suffered, the torment of bullies at school, the realization of unfairness, the desire for acceptance, and the negative feelings of unrealized expectations. All the contents add up to the image you have of yourself. When you go *fishing,* which

5

Figure 1.1   How Clean Is Your Lake?

experiences are most likely to be reeled in? Probably those tied to your deepest desires or fears, the ones that have the greatest impact on how you see yourself. It is these experiences that create the image you call *you*. Your self-esteem (how you feel about yourself) and your self-worth (the value you place on yourself in comparison to others) come from the depth of these waters. Most of us can honestly say we do not have the cleanest, most pristine body of mental thoughts to fish from (see Figure 1.1).

Your workplace personality is the mirror image of your self-image. It determines how you act in front of your co-workers and how you thrive and compete in the organizational culture.

 Your thoughts shape your self-image.

WHERE DID THAT THOUGHT COME FROM?

When we communicate with others, we are bringing forth from our minds (our lakes) the reality created by us or for us, one that may be very different than the reality the coworker/listener is operating in. Think of the words in your vocabulary. Where did they come from? Who do they belong to? You? What if I told you that you do not own any words! None of the words you present with authority belong to you, nor were they devised by your incredible imaginations. When you were born, you were given a *platter of words* meant to define your specific circumstances of birth: male, female, black, white, cute, ugly, rich, poor, privileged, untouchable, and so on. As you moved through life, in and out of experiences, relationships, jobs, careers, you amassed more and more words and labels, claiming and accepting them as your own. Did you choose these words, these labels? No, you did not, but you did quickly agree and conform to them. We all did. We did not understand that, from the beginning of the process of enculturation, we had a choice. The Sapir-Whorf hypothesis (named for Benjamin L. Whorf and Edward Sapir) is a linguistic "mould theory" that seeks to explain the impact of language on the individual, and how this impact, though very personal, is a shared experience for all humankind. In essence it states that *language equals social reality.* The words you use, most of them added to the language before you were born, have been assigned to you to define and determine how you should see and experience life (see Figure 1.2).

For example, think about the many Inuit words for snow versus the absence of the same word/phenomenon in the world of the Maasai tribe of Kenya. Different realities create different degrees of relevance for different words. What type of reality do your words come from? What words have been assigned to you in the workplace: boss, supervisor, worker, CEO, janitor, secretary? What adjectives: smart, clever, persistent or lazy, dull?

7

© PS Perkins - 2005

Platter Analogy - Life Is Served!

Figure 1.2 Your Words Served Up!

CREATING OUR SELF-IMAGE AT WORK

I remember an interview on *Larry King Live* in 1999 with the successful magicians and illusionists Siegfried and Roy. They were both discussing their childhood and their later ascent to fame. Siegfried talked about how his big break came after he left home. Apparently, his childhood was filled with negative *mirror messages*—the messages we receive about ourselves from others—and very little positive attention from his father. He said it was not until he was a very successful illusionist that his father ever really talked with him or acknowledged any aspect of his worth. Siegfried shared how troubling this was for him as a young man. His story is not unlike the story of millions who possess the residue of negative messages they have floating in their lake. The messages are the material we use to create our self-image and self-worth. However, a fortunate few break through the cycle of negativity and create new agreements in their lives. This is what Siegfried had to do, to break free of the thoughts, words, memories that might have kept him from realizing his full potential and his unique gift, the career of a lifetime.

Think about the attention paid to personal image and how we are programmed (especially by Western culture) to be very

8

image conscious. The perception of beauty is often narrowly defined, and we all dream of looking like a fashion model or fitness expert. Day in and day out, we are inundated with the pictures of the "preferable" images of beauty, the ones that equate with success and acceptability. Watching this, what type of messages must we be dredging from our lakes on a daily basis?

Ever wonder what your colleagues think about your looks, your dress, and other appearance factors? How about when you have to address an audience? How much of stage fright is precipitated by your concerns over what others will think about you and especially how you look? Be honest. So many individuals in the organizational environment sabotage themselves from the inside out. Daily, I consult with business professionals who block, stall, or lose opportunities within their organizations due to poor self-image and the fear or inability to effectively communicate their abilities. This is a major problem for many individuals climbing the corporate ladder. They think about themselves and see themselves in a manner that does not foster professional success. Take for instance the societal phenomenon in which everyone compares herself to everyone else—*social comparison.* How does the cultural norm of social comparisons affect the work environment?

Many of us remember the sociocultural phrase "keeping up with the Joneses." You know the Joneses, the successful family that lives on the top of the hill in the big white house, with the picket fence and two-car garage—Lexus and BMW inside—and the 2.5 kids. Think about how the cultural value of *individualism,* with the resultant *competition,* drives the vast majority of people to look outward and compare themselves with everyone around them. Examine the impact of these values on the work environment and on how you gauge your position and relationship to others there. For many, comparison leads to constantly questioning their professional self-worth. There is this constant nagging voice to look at what everyone else is doing or whether you are getting your just due. Of course, the habit is not just a Western phenomenon. It's a condition of being human, exaggerated in some cultures based on the need of a given society to move in one direction or the other. In the West, the value of competition makes the habit very strong indeed, and in doing so accounts for a significant portion of the feelings of inadequacy many individuals experience in and out of the workplace. As a result, millions conform to their work surroundings in a manner that *protects* their position. But the question is how does this conformity affect you personally? Do you experience professional fulfillment based on your unique contributions to the organizational objective? Do you fit the ideal and are thus able to experience the rewards of such conformity within the professional environment? Are you allowed to really impact the organizational mission? Not everyone finds it easy to "get in" or "fit in." Read Sheila's story.

GROWING UP "DIFFERENT"

Growing up in what I considered to be a stable, middle-class African-American family, I hold the memory of my early life as far back as three and four years old. My family and my community in these early recollections were a reflection of me. I was born in the Southern United States before the end of Jim Crow—government-sanctioned segregation. As such, I grew up in a self-contained environment, socially, religiously, and politically. Only employment took us from our safe havens. The messages I received in my community were messages of being smart, talented, and accepted. My early world was one of homogeneity. Everyone was a reflection of me. The occasional Euro-American came by in the form of bill collectors or the "vegetable man."

My parents were considered highly educated "Negroes." My father acquired an undergraduate degree from a famed historically black college, in music, and then went on to receive a Master's in English from a recognized prestigious university. My mother was a registered nurse by trade. Her father was the owner of a neighborhood grocery store and restaurant, and his father had the fortune of being one of the first "coloreds" to work for a prestigious bank in other than a custodial capacity. My father's father was a Mason and a Shriner, my grandmother a member of the Daughters of Isis and a Morning Star. As children, we were members of Jack and Jill, a philanthropic community-support network of parents. These affiliations meant little to me as a child, but would later become very relevant in the formation of my self-image and self-worth. These were the collective experiences of family and community.

In the fifth grade, I was bused to a predominantly white school. I was anxious, scared, but excited about the prospect of going to a new school with "different" people, and that difference seemed to be something special as far as I had observed. By this time the images of television, magazines, and other representations of mass media had already begun to give me the distinct awareness of being different, and for some reason I began to equate this with *undesirable*.

On the first day at my new school, one of my first contacts was with two little White girls who sent a clear message on the playground during recess. They chanted, "Look at those ugly, black legs. We don't want to see those skinny, black legs. Why don't you cover them up?" (Yes, I remember the words. They were quickly added to my *lake* of experiences.) I was in shock! I ran to tell the teacher, who gently chided their "playful antics." The quality of the water in my lake was changing. The messages I was now receiving were not as affirming; they were meant to distinguish me from others who had their places of privilege already carved out. I did not belong.

Unfortunately, these early experiences became a part of my lake of experiences and I started to create a self-image of *victim*. My lake was becoming a cauldron of contradictions and mixed messages. Now don't get me wrong: I was experiencing nonaffirming messages from some around me. I did experience racism and sexism firsthand. But it was I and only I who made the decision to keep these messages in my lake and feed on them as I moved among my real and imagined persecutors! I often blamed "them" for the job I did not get. I often second-guessed the ulterior motives of my colleagues when *my* idea was not chosen. I would carry the perceived injuries around with me all day long, looking for the next insult to my ability or intelligence to pounce on me! It was a way of life that kept me frustrated, cynical, mistrusting, and often depressed. Now, I know this paints a pretty bleak picture, but I learned to play the "no problem" game pretty well with everyone but myself, so the baggage was visible and heavy only on my back! The true self does not lie. I was angry and it was somebody else's fault. Did I advance at work? Sure I did. The *victim game* made me pretty competitive, gave me an "I'll show them" type of mentality. I wore the mask of accomplishment and contentment pretty well on the job, and was highly productive, but it was my self-talk that clearly defined my true nature. I would go in my office and close the door, or go home in the evening, and engage in a never-ceasing mental dialogue about some verbal injury or about being overlooked, or you name it—it did not take much for me to enter into my victim mind-set. I was not happy, because I made myself unhappy with thoughts that constantly dwelled on past injustices and expected future slights. I realized, and thankfully not too late, that there needed to be a change and that change had to come from me!

What's your story? Is it different than Sheila's? Was growing up inside your household a challenging experience and you escaped into the outside world to get away? Were the messages you received from your caretakers the ones that damaged your self-esteem? What messages are you still regurgitating to your own harm? Who are you still blaming? What experiences sit at your desk with you each day, fueling unhealthy thoughts, words, and actions? How clean is the water in your lake?

WRITING A NEW SCRIPT

After those formative years, Sheila engaged in the positive reformation of her self-identification, self-esteem, and self-worth. She waged a difficult but increasingly successful battle to reprogram the words and the messages that had been particularly destructive to her physical, mental, emotional, and spiritual health. She has made great progress in overcoming the scavengers at the bottom of the lake. She has examined her personal responsibility and adopted an attitude of worthiness and capability regardless of any lingering messages to the contrary from her past or the people around her. In order to live in real peace and fulfillment, personally or professionally, we must all be willing to engage in this level of self-examination.

We must not fear our own truth.

Do not be afraid to look within.
The ego tells you all is black with guilt within you, and bids you
   not to look.
Instead, it bids you to look upon your brothers, and see the guilt
   in them.
Yet this you cannot do without remaining blind.

A Course in Miracles

Victory can be yours in conquering whatever messages have been the caustic agents of embitterment, discouragement, and destruction in your own life. How are the scavengers in your lake trying to prevent you from coming into your personal and professional power? Understand the illusion of their hold on your life. Name them but do not claim them!

Maybe you just need to skim a couple of thoughts floating on the top of your lake. Maybe you need a water-filtering system. Maybe you need to dig a completely new lake. We must begin to see how our thoughts about ourselves have been our greatest allies or our greatest nemeses in creating the self-image that becomes our *work image*.

TAKING OWNERSHIP

We need to understand a fundamental truth concerning language: "He who owns the words, owns everything." As described before, on a platter before you are all the words you will need to fit into the prescribed place that society has already marked out for you. But you do not have the understanding to examine or question this platter; you just start eating. The feast includes all the words concerning your self-identification—the way you see yourself and the manner in which you will live your life. The words describe your sex, gender, ethnicity, looks, social status, economics, opportunities, and so forth. No one cautions you to examine each word before you eat. Why not? Because they never examined the words put in front of them! Everyone around you is still absorbing the words on their platters, living up to the identities carved out for them. For far too many, these word choices are limiting, debilitating, and visionless.

You must take control over the words you use to create your daily images of self and others. I have examined the words presented to me on the platter of life and now am much more discerning about what I eat. If you do not take the time to define yourself, there are others lined up to do it for you. If you do not know who you are, there will be many others always ready to tell you *who you are not!* A famous quote by Winston Churchill best illustrates the power of being narrator of your own life: "History will be kind to me, for I intend to write it."

14

Behavioral Communication practitioners describe this process as *metacognition*—the ability to think about what you are thinking about. To cleanse your thoughts, you need to examine them. The work includes *self-monitoring*—the ability to watch your thoughts shape themselves, to understand how given thoughts will show up negatively or positively in your personal situation, and to deliberately choose to change course or move forward in the desired direction. This is a vital tool for understanding change as it happens in the moment. Too many of us go home from work and dredge up from our lake all the toxic waste of the workday, then spew it into the home environment. You know how the rest of the story goes.

I will never forget a young client who was introduced to the concept of self-monitoring. One day he came into a session with a stopwatch hanging around his neck. He was dressed in a business suit, so I knew he could not have come from the gym. I decided to ignore it and move into the session, until I heard this incessant clicking. At several intervals during our coaching session, he would click the stopwatch. Finally, I asked him what was going on. He replied, "I am monitoring my negative thoughts." It took me a minute to understand. He went on to share, "Yeah, when I understood the importance of self-monitoring, I started to count the number of times my thoughts would turn against me. I could not keep up with it and was getting a bit discouraged. So I got this stopwatch to keep tabs on the number of negative thoughts I was having. Guess what? When I first started clicking, I could not believe that I was experiencing up to three hundred and something negative thoughts a day! Now I am down to a few dozen!" As his coach, I was astounded by his effort, diligence, and honesty. Admittedly, the stopwatch may have been a little drastic for his social and professional environments, but you have to admit, he got the idea!

What thoughts and words have been placed on your platter without your permission? What toxic images have you ingested without understanding the repercussions? Take a moment to try Application 1.1.

Application 1.1 - Monitor Your Thoughts

Make a list of all the words you use to describe yourself.

Go ahead, write them down. Describe your gender, looks, body image, skin color, class, religion. Every word you can think of that constitutes a label you attach to yourself. After you assemble the list, ask yourself, "Did I make up these words? Did I choose these labels for myself?" Which words empower you? Which words limit you? Which images have you struggled to throw off? Which words have you readily accepted, and to your detriment or benefit?

For each of us, our words create a different movie that has become the story of our lives (more about that later). What would it take for you to rid yourself of words on your platter that are not creating the type of life you want to star in? Believe me: it's as simple as choosing different words. Monitor your thoughts BEFORE they become your words and then actions. Create a new platter!

Did you take the time to go through Application 1.1 and really examine the quality of thoughts and words you are using every day, the thoughts and words that create your communication environment? Is it time to make some changes? Does the water in your lake need a serious filtering system installed? Are you making momentary critical choices concerning the manner in which you formulate your thoughts: which words become yours, which actions become yours, which life becomes your life? Remember, unchecked thoughts lead to unchecked words that lead to uncontrollable chaos. Understandably, many will find it difficult at first to monitor their thoughts consistently. One method that will help is to be in constant touch with your feelings. How do you *feel* on a day-to-day basis? Good? Bad? Indifferent? These *feelings* will attest to whether or not you are in control of your thoughts. Bad feelings are a clear signal that there are negative thoughts trying to invade your lake—your well-being. You will probably find that there are negative thoughts and words accompanying these feelings. If you do not feed the negative feelings, they will disappear. Replace the negative feelings, thoughts, and words with more empowering, positive feelings, thoughts, and words. Sing! Laugh! Pray! Dance!

Review the agreements you have made that cast you as a character in someone else's vision of your life. Examine the socialization/enculturation process you have gone through that holds you captive. The *self-fulfilling prophecies* of your life come from the real you, deep inside at the bottom of the lake. You have to go fishing and dredge up all the thoughts, experiences, and people that need to be cast away. Discontinue the consistent drama of comparing yourself to others and creating the endless cycle of dissatisfaction, the need for outside approval.

Engage in Application 1.2 to help re-create the life you want to live.

Application 1.2 - Dreambook to Success

Use a scrapbook or spiral notebook to gather together a living journal filled with your hopes, dreams, and desires for today, tomorrow, the future.

Fill it with positive sayings, new agreements you want to make with yourself, pictures of places where you would like to travel, possessions you would like to own, and relationships you would like to experience. Do not just concentrate on the material desires but imagine the type of people and experiences you want to have.

I call this a "Dreambook" and it's used to create a new dream for your life. I have experienced the manifestation of many desires within my Dreambook over the last few years. I am adding to my Dreambook frequently, finally taking control of my own destiny, actively participating in its materialization. It has been a life-altering, astounding experience to see my self-fulfilling prophecy at work.

JILL'S DAY

Let's return to the woman we met in the beginning pages of the book. We all witnessed Jill's workday get under way as she solidly placed her feet on the floor and moved into deliberate consciousness. Do you remember Situation #1, her first conscious thoughts about being late and not going to the cleaners? What was her mental breakfast, the mental fuel that started her day? Here we have a clear example of waking up on the wrong side of the bed, and of how the lack of a deliberate choice to make a change in attitude can greatly affect the rest of the day. It is the same experience you are having on too many days. But brighter days are just ahead.

What Jill did not understand was that it was her first thoughts that determined the rest of her day! What may seem like a simple irritant is enough to create massive frustration. The energy behind realizing she forgot her clothes at the cleaners became the same energy that set the rest of her day in motion. The energy began to take a shape and momentum of its own. It followed her to the bathroom, where she broke her nail on the cabinet as she slammed the door. It caught up with her as she cursed herself for forgetting to pick up the milk for cereal for the kids. While driving to work, she was thinking about her relationship with Don and how their marriage had become so mundane. In the process, she almost ran the red light! I hope you are getting the point. Once the energy begins to build, like attracts like. Jill's self-talk, her Intrapersonal Communication, consistently determined her outlook throughout the workday, in every communication experience. From the moment she drove into the parking lot and began negative self-talk about Richard, to her first encounter, to scheduled meetings, to the decisions she made and the conflict she resolved, it all came back to how she began her day and the interaction she had with herself *about* herself and others.

This is why the first step of the communication model is so vital. Everything hinges on your ability to begin each day in a way that will produce the results you desire. The essential key is to understand that the present thought determines the present moment. This is why we often hear various teachers and philosophies mandate the need to "stay in the moment," "focus on the present," or "remain in the now." This exhortation is based on the simple truth that each moment stands alone. Often times, the *now* is marred and tainted by one's preoccupation with past moments or the unforeseen future, neither of which can create a contented and rich present! Understanding the fundamental position of Intrapersonal Communication as the origin of all other communication experiences is the essential key to workplace success.

In reading Jill's story we see how throughout the day she kept going back to the residue of dissatisfaction and discontent. Additionally, she consistently propelled herself forward to "what ifs."

WAKING UP TO YOUR DAY!

How do you typically get up each morning? Do you purposefully direct your thoughts? Try it. How much of your moment-to-moment thoughts are filled with past worry, unfocused expectations at work, anger, thoughts of defeat, self-doubt? These are the seeds that are germinating and producing the fruit of your present moment and, if you're not careful, all future moments! Plant healthy seeds of thought, fertilize with affirmative words, and grow positive experiences. When gardening, we understand the science of a healthy plant. Well, the *garden* of the mind is no different. It is where you create the experiences of your life. Think of your mind as fertile soil where your thoughts are the seeds that grow your life.

Seed + fertilizer + water = fruit

It is the same as saying . . .

19

Thoughts + Communication + Actions = Your Life

CONQUERING THE FIRST STEP

You are more than a conqueror! Lack of awareness and under-standing is the first major obstacle to overcome. Once you are aware of the science of Intrapersonal Communication and un-derstand its relationship to your life, you are ready to start the process of changing the world around you from inside out! And that start is where you stand right now. Individuals at-tempting to transform their lives by the renewing of their minds often feel overwhelmed by the task. Resist the urge to fall backward or leap ahead. Resist the temptation to dwell on the difficulties of reprogramming your thoughts. Replace the doubts of "can't do" with "can do" and "will do"! The power is within you to think what YOU want to think, not what others tell you to think or how others think. Do not fall into the trap of "this is too hard" or "I do not have the time." It is a matter of enjoying an abundant life or suffering an agonizing, unful-filled life!

FIRST THINGS FIRST!

Start your day off the way you intend for it to go. As you begin to awaken while still lying quietly, purposefully greet the day with mental and verbal objectives, realistic expectations, and heartfelt thanksgivings. See yourself moving forward through your workday in the manner you wish to be received. Contem-plate the attitude and actions you will exhibit as you think pos-itively and constructively through your day *before* you hit the floor running. And there's another important point: stop running! It is the hurry-up attitude that has us all consistently scrambling away from where we are supposed to be—in the moment.

Personal responsibility for our own success and happiness is not a framework that is easy to work from in a world where what happens is too often everybody else's fault. Think about it. Are you both successful and happy? If you are living in the same frame of mind as most people, I dare say not. Most people will sacrifice one quality for the other because they feel, or have been told, that they must do so. Often, due to the pressures of financial needs and wants, we sacrifice happiness for an empty shell of financial success. But guess what, we can have it all! We all have the power to create that abundant life once we fully connect with our individual genius and the action required to manifest our genius. The wonderful writer and theologian Frederick Buechner shared with his students the formula for having a life of both success and happiness:

"To find your mission in life is to discover the intersection between your heart's deep gladness and the world's deep hunger."

Dare to move your professional goals into direct alignment both with your unique passion and with a need the world has. This may be where you are presently planted, or it may be your next garden of cultivation. Either way, you were born to manifest the genius within. Doing so starts with your ability to merge the thoughts of your creative mind with the words you speak, that create what you actualize. Speak words that help you to experience your work environment as fulfilling. "In the beginning was the WORD!" The first step is to understand the communication patterns that will positively affect every step you take thereafter. Below you will find a synopsis of how the first step of Intrapersonal Communication will help ensure your professional success and happiness.

Adopt these Intrapersonal Communication strategies through-out your communication workday:

Understand how the *science* of communication goes far beyond an ability to talk.

- With each thought, with each word, you create actions that turn into the life you are living.

Understand that communication begins on the inside and determines the outside.

- Take the first step to begin a new attitude of personal responsibility for the thoughts you are thinking. They cannot dwell there unless you invite them to stay.

Clean out your lake—engage in a thorough examination of your thoughts and words and fill your lake with new agreements about yourself and others.

- You must replace old doubts, fears, resentments, frustration, and anger with a renewed sense of self-worth, with self-love. Dr. Martin Luther King Jr. was quoted as saying, "No one can ride your back unless it is bent!" Straighten up!

- Forgive yourself, forgive others, and move on up! Forgiveness allows you to remember the lesson without the anger or other negative emotions.

 Don't forget the lesson, just let go of the attachment.

Use affirmations, meditation, prayer.

- Seek out pearls of wisdom and write them in a journal, on note cards, or in your Dreambook. Place the affirmations in locations where you will see and read them daily—the nightstand, your mirror, fridge, or desk. The wonderful thing about affirmations is they are there to confirm our dreams and goals. Don't just read them, but speak them aloud!

 We are all materializing the world around us through our thoughts, words, and deeds. Some are doing it intentionally and some are not!

Application 1.3 will help you understand the way affirmations can work for you throughout your day.

- Meditate on the vision you have for your life. Remember Descartes: "Except our own thoughts, there is nothing absolutely in our power." Think of your passion as if it already is!

- Prayer is a consistent conversation with that which is universal creativity. I have found that a very appropriate

Application 1.3 - Affirmations Work!

Exchange nonaffirming thoughts with affirming thoughts and statements.

⊖ I hate my job!	⊕ I look forward to a more rewarding experience at work and my career!
⊖ I can't stand my boss!	⊕ I would prefer a more understanding boss, but I appreciate his vision.
⊖ I wish I was thin.	⊕ I appreciate my personality and know that my outer-person does not define me. I am working toward a healthier me!

No, the affirmations do not solve the issues. But they create a mind that can!

use of prayer is to seek those characteristics and gifts that help us to make the right choices, whether personally, socially, or professionally.

Practice self-monitoring.

- As discussed earlier in the chapter, this Intrapersonal Communication tool allows you to be right there in the moment, involved in making choices as to your thoughts and resultant words. I cannot think of a more helpful tool to use at work. "Think before you speak!"

Practice self-management.

- As you enter your work environment, you immediately start to reaffirm the image you carry around of yourself at work. By understanding the connection between your external work environment and your internal processes of communication, you are assured of greater personal fulfillment and professional communication success.

Remember the lesson of "Be, Do, Have."

- Here's one approach to life: If I *have* a nice ride, I will *do* my thing by driving around town so everyone can see me, and then I will *be* somebody and everyone will know it.

- This formula bases self-worth in possessions. Self-esteem is replaced by social esteem.

- A better formula: If I (be) am successful in managing my mind, in choosing my thoughts and words, I will do things—make choices, take actions—that resonate with success. They will cause me to attract success and thereby have it. If I (be) am kind, I will do kind things and have kindness in return. The formula can be applied to millions of scenarios, but the outcome is ALWAYS the same:

24

You cannot have and keep what you are not!

You have successfully begun your journey up the staircase by accepting the key part that self-understanding plays in your communication IQ. Our next step is to understand the role our nonverbal messages play in determining the outcome of our communication with others.

Do you realize that as much as 93 percent of your trust and believability is communicated through nonverbal communication? Within personal or professional settings, NVC accounts for the majority of your communication. Are you ready to climb the second step to greater communication confidence and power?

"I am what I think I am. My thoughts are not separate from me."

Q & A Intrapersonal Communication

Dear PS,

Q: I'm always wondering what others think about me at work.

A: It's funny; they are probably having the same thoughts. The important thing is to understand how you think about yourself. Remember, everyone sees you as *you* see yourself. Create a positive self-image and you will not be concerned about how others see you, only that you are true to yourself.

Q: I have a colleague who consistently talks negatively about her job and the company. How can I help her change her outlook?

A: Are you her supervisor or an acquaintance? Your relationship with her will determine your course of action. If you are a person responsible for addressing and evaluating job performance, seek support from company staff-development programs that focus on professional enrichment. Talk with her about her unrealized aspirations and how she can engage in an assertive push to position herself where she wants to be. Offer support.

Q: I have a colleague who is so negative. She always wants to have lunch together but all she does is gripe and complain about the job and gossip about coworkers.

A: As a colleague, this may be more sensitive and you need to determine the importance of the friendship and your level of involvement with her as it affects the job. Be clear that you value your work environment and seek to be content and productive while at work. Ask if there is anything you can do to help her achieve the same. Offer her self-help books and guides to encourage her to a more positive self-image. If she does not respond positively to your help and concern, have lunch with someone else.

Q: I can't seem to leave my personal problems behind while I'm at work. It's really affecting my job performance.

A: Worry can be a major distraction for all of us. It can become a debilitating habit that impacts all areas of one's life. But understand a very important truth: worry stems from a past experience you have not let go of, and/or from a future imagined experience that has not happened. Only the present offers true success and contentment. Train your mind to stay focused on the moment. You will become much more productive and able to solve any challenge at the time it presents itself. Bend your circumstances to your mind, not your mind to your circumstances.

Q: I have been overlooked for several promotions at work. As a result my self-esteem is very low!

A: Are you sure it isn't the other way around? Your low self-esteem may be creating an image that does not come across as promotable. Search your private lake of experiences. Does your self-image present an individual who is "in-charge"? The public image we present of ourselves may not actually be the way we see ourselves. But the *real* you always shines through. Speak to a respected colleague for an honest assessment of why opportunities are passing you by. Seek a professional coach or take a class in communication that will help you more closely analyze the personal blockages to your professional goals. If you honestly feel that you are promotable but that office politics is getting in the way, have a frank discussion with your supervisor at an appropriate time and setting, and ask for an honest assessment of your future within the department, suggestions for how to improve your chances, and a realistic time line for your expectations. Honest communication with yourself and others is ALWAYS the answer! You just have to be ready to really listen.

Q: I am what some call a "minority" at work. My ethnic background is not of the dominant culture. I constantly feel singled out about my work, my accent, my clothes. I feel like I experience greater scrutiny than most of my coworkers but work twice as hard.

A: You are a prime candidate for the work we are doing in this book. Read Chapter 1 and reread it, again and again. Seek out other professionals who can relate to the personal and professional concerns of being a member of a coculture within the dominant culture workforce. Read Chapter 7 on Intercultural Communication and apply the tools needed for Cross-cultural Communication effectiveness. Make an honest assessment of yourself and seek out and destroy the *victim*. Then move forward in the confidence of the unique gifts you can contribute to the work environment. Employ the aid of mentors and professional development to help you navigate the organizational culture. Offer input as to how the organization can move from lip service to true inclusion. Demographics and the global workforce are mandating more inclusive work environments. You can be a catalyst for change. But first: "Be the change you want to see."

Nonverbal Communication

"A picture is worth a thousand words."

—American expression

THE FUNCTIONS OF NONVERBAL COMMUNICATION

I hate the way he looks through me like I don't exist. He always shakes my hand like a wet fish! And every time he comes near me, that cologne! Yuck!"

You probably remember reading these thoughts from Jill in the introduction as she thinks about her colleague Richard. How many of the above references have to do with nonverbal perceptions? Nonverbal Communication, or NVC, is defined as *the messages we send and receive from others without words, both on a conscious and subconscious level.* In understanding that communication can be unintentional as well as intentional, and that *unintentional* communication is often derived from NVC, we see the large role Nonverbal Communication plays in the dynamics of how people relate to one another in the workplace. This second step in communication awareness is a large part of the lake we discussed in the last chapter.

The thoughts you express as words and emotions become your habits, which feed your nonverbal language—the manner in which you nonverbally express yourself.

We learn the nonverbal codes of a society much in the same way we learn language, as an integral part of our symbol system. Just as with language, we do not always acquire the most effective nonverbal habits. The messages come from the inside out and are reinforced by others around us, generally using the same set of agreed-upon symbol systems put in place by the dominant members of the culture. We take this same set of communication skills, rules, and expectations into the organizational setting.

Every culture or society has a set of nonverbal messages that are taught and learned by its members to organize a multitude of embedded symbols for the purpose of creating society and maintaining order. All cultures have separately developed nonverbal messages based on their collective realities. These symbols create the reality of the dominant culture, a reality further enhanced by symbols created by the cocultures within the society, who through their language patterns and experiences create alternative realities.

More than your verbal message—the actual words you speak—there are thousands of nonverbal messages you send and receive every day. What type of messages do you send, consciously and unconsciously, in the way you dress, your facial expression, your greeting rituals, your displays of emotion, your gestures, your tone of voice, or your use of space? When speaking of Nonverbal Communication, many automatically think "body language," but NVC is much more than the messages we relay through our physical bodies. A variety of studies, such as the one done at the University of California–Los Angeles by Professor Albert Mehrabian in his classic NVC work, have concluded:

- 7 percent of meaning is in the words that are spoken.
- 38 percent of meaning is paralinguistic (the way that the words are said).
- 55 percent of meaning is in the visual message, such as facial expression.

These statistics reveal that the nonverbal messages we send, and not the words we speak, account for as much as 93 percent of the messages others receive from us when judging our level of trust and believability. Nonverbal messages can be broken down into visual, vocal, physical, and spatial messages. There are several arenas of NVC we operate within all day. Indeed, such communication is a vast field of study that is a primary consideration in many areas of human exploration, including the workplace, architecture, interior design, medicine, education, physical science, behavioral science, organizational behavior, and landscaping. We are vastly more than the words we speak, which are often a cover for how we really feel and experience life. How many times do you say one thing and mean another, or experience others manipulating NVC for a desired gain? An example would be dressing professionally for an interview. We talk to one another loudly in the gestures we use, the space we maintain, and the eyes that reveal all!

We use Nonverbal Communication, consciously and subconsciously, to fulfill seven (7) varied functions: (1) to substitute words, (2) to control the impression others have of us, (3) to complement the words we speak, (4) to contradict our words, (5) to confirm the messages of others, (6) to distinguish relationships between ourselves and others, and (7) to maintain a congruent understanding of the messages within a shared environment (such as the workplace). These seven factors are how we generally interact with colleagues at work.

Think for a minute about the nonverbal patterns found in the United States and the agreed-upon gestures for "stop," "OK," "hello," "goodbye," smiling, and frowning. How about our recognition of space as a way to denote power? Or what about the nonverbal rituals of what is appropriate and inappropriate touching, and how much of an impact touching rituals play in the discussion of appropriate versus inappropriate touching at work? How about the use of color in its ritualistic uses of business versus social or weddings versus funerals? Examples can be seen in the white of a doctor's office or black worn at a funeral. All of these issues are determined by our agreed-upon symbol system of NVC. Notice that as we move into our various communication experiences, we conform to the specific verbal and nonverbal patterns of the environment. We go to work and adopt the jargon, symbols, and appropriate NVC of the organizational culture. These symbols are embedded within the social realities of all distinct cultures, usually greatly influenced by the historical and religious underpinnings of the culture.

NVC is a major factor in all cultures but within its own culture-specific context of appearance, paralanguage, kinesics, chronemics, proxemics, haptics, and olfactory. As we discuss these variables, remember that Nonverbal Communication is *culturally bound:* its symbols change from culture to culture. We will examine these NVC arenas as they appear in the U.S. workplace culture (see Figure 2.1).

YOUR PROFESSIONAL APPEARANCE

Appearance is the first of our nonverbal codes to examine. It is the *outer image you present to the world according to prescribed societal and workplace constructs.* All cultures have what we call a standard of physical beauty and acceptance that most members of the culture aspire to. Studies have been done that identify the common denominator of beauty for most hu-

© PS Perkins – 2007

Figure 2.1 Nonverbal Communication Areas

mans as symmetry of the body, specifically the symmetry of facial features. Obviously, appearance is an important factor in the communication exchange of humans. Do individuals notice a person's sex, skin color, or apparel as the person makes a first impression? It of course depends on the person and how they were socialized to process these attributes. We have all heard the adage "don't judge a book by its cover." But let's face it; that is exactly what we do each day when we meet and engage people in the workplace. Only a very small percentage of the people we meet on a daily basis become players in our *movie*, due to what attracts us to one another or the circumstances that compel us together, such as work.

What areas of physical appearance do you tend to pay a lot of attention to? Some look for a nice smile. Others say the eyes are the windows to the soul. Some love to see a man in an expensive suit with nice shoes. Some love gray hair around the temples. Tall, short, plump, thin . . . the lists of likes and dislikes are endless, but the point is that we are an image-obsessed culture. Your image, your visual impression, is very important, especially in a youth- and beauty-conscious culture such as the United States. This is also the major communication arena within which *social comparisons* often operate.

Appearance in the workplace is often used as an indicator of appropriateness, professionalism, and position within the organizational setting. Growing up, I remember my father being one of those "blue suit" guys with IBM. It was a part of the culture. Many institutions have prescribed dress codes, but there are many that don't, and the variable of diversity adds a lot to the cultural appearance factor. We live in times where Middle Eastern and Arab dress is often met with stereotyping, prejudice, and fear. We live in times where Western dress is sometimes viewed by other cultures as too revealing. The workplace brings these dress mores together. How do you perceive yourself in this area of communication? Are you acutely aware of the nonverbal messages you send and receive all day through something as personal as your physical appearance?

I often work with individuals from urban communities who have adopted patterns of dress that identify their unique brand of seeing and experiencing the world. This sometimes includes apparel such as very low-riding pants, untied sneakers, hair wraps, flip-flops, baggy shorts, and tattoos. Many would say that this would not be considered the appropriate attire for professional setting. To these youth, it is a way of expression that identifies their unique experiences. Many of you reading this book have already conformed to the prescriptions put forth by the dominant culture of what is acceptable patterns of appearance, as well as what is considered culturally beautiful. There are many who are willing to take whatever measures necessary to be considered *desirable*.

One of my favorite episodes from *The Twilight Zone,* the program hosted by Rod Serling, was about a young woman who was going through her eleventh medical procedure to alter her facial appearance to meet societal standards. In this particular conformist culture, it was a crime to look different. (Rod Serling was a master of social commentary, using *Twilight Zone* episodes as a cover to tackle some of the complex and sensitive social issues of his time.) When the bandages were removed, the operation was unsuccessful and the patient was to be transferred to a colony to live with people of "her own kind." The genius of the episode lay in the fact that the viewer was never given a straight-on look at the faces of the hospital staff, only shadows and glimpses of body parts. When the results of the surgery were in and the "lights were turned on," we see that the *normal* people have faces that are contorted and deformed, all alike for the sake of conformity. The patient was transferred to a colony with "people of her own kind." The episode is entitled "Eye of the Beholder." Its messages are as clear and relevant today as they were in 1960.

Many remain in a constant state of dissatisfaction because they never seem to measure up to the ideal. Approval issues, such as image in the workplace, also hurt the organization's bottom line in the amount of money and human capital lost because of time devoted to cosmetic surgery, cosmetic dentistry, spas, nail and hair salons, and so on. Maybe we need to look at this very factor affecting business productivity and how we can create more inclusive environments.

This can be particularly difficult in the competitive arena of work. In our patriarchal culture, white males dominate the corporate decision-making body. As a result, their paradigms of appropriate versus inappropriate dress are the standardized dress codes of the workplace. There are many experiences that have been documented about various organizations adopting dress code mandates specifically aimed at a particular cultural pattern—proscriptions such as no facial hair, no braids, no locks, no long nails, no head wraps, and so on. These dress codes are made to make "some" individuals more comfortable and accepted than others. A better paradigm of inclusion would be to foster organizational environments that encourage apparel distinction that is

35

culturally expressive yet professional. If the "look" is in no way a hindrance to work productivity, what's the problem?

How can we see and appreciate uniqueness, yet at the same time be able to effectively compete in a work culture that too often offers very narrow prescriptions of professional image? Part of my self-healing process has been the need to re-define and reprogram the concept of beauty I was programmed to believe in. You must do the same. If you presently fit the ideal, still realize it is not all that you are. Beauty does fade, especially if it is totally based on outward appearances. For those of us constantly finding ourselves having to compete in the appearance game, often accumulating more and more stuff to satiate the desire to fit in, it's high time to create a new paradigm.

No longer judge yourself by the narrow, shallow definition of beauty and its accoutrements. Broaden your definition. Just like you try new foods and acquire new tastes, do the same with your prescriptions of beauty. Do not allow Gucci, Pucci, Larucci, or Fubu to be a measurement by which you define your self-worth. But always remember, communication—whether it is verbal or nonverbal, such as with appearance—is appropriate or inappropriate, never good or bad. This is a very important point. Communication is always based on the realities of the sender and the receiver. The closer the shared realities, the more likely the shared symbols will be congruent and thus more compatible.

So, getting back to the young urban hip-hop dresser, enjoy your uniqueness but understand that all communication is governed by setting, time, and place. Take an inventory of how you present your professional best in terms of the work environment. Appearance sets the stage! Are you satisfied to just mirror everyone else or do you adopt an attitude of personal excellence? Based on the setting, you may need to adopt a more conservative dress style for the workplace. Maybe you need to be more relaxed or *season* stylish. Extend your considerations about your wardrobe beyond clothes to nails, hair, colors, shoe types, and other complements that can greatly affect the visual image. And, of course, it never hurts to get a second opinion from someone we trust or from an expert when trying to find the right look. Rule of thumb: When in Rome, do as the Romans; when at home, do as the homeys! Make your communication appropriate for the setting to win the prize you are seeking—a promising career path.

YOUR PROFESSIONAL VOICE

Our next NVC code is *paralanguage*. Paralanguage is not *what* you say, but *how* you say what you say. It is the vocal qualities that surround your words. It is tone, pitch, emphasis, stress, inflection, volume, pacing, accent, dialect, pausing, silence, and a host of other vocal variables unique only to you. However, every culture has prescriptions for what sounds pleasing, professional, educated, or illiterate. These often act as a way of categorizing people and even stereotyping some. This can be especially detrimental in the workplace.

I have worked with dozens of individuals trying to "fix" their speaking voices to come more in line with prescribed patterns of acceptance. This is basically the General American accent we hear on national broadcast networks. I have worked with individuals seeking accent reduction, dialect reduction, volume increase/decrease, projection, help with stuttering, lisp, nasality, and so on. There have been times when an employee will share that a promotion has been stalled time and time again because of the lack of authority in the employee's voice, or because of a cultural accent that the employer feels will be a detriment to supervisory authority. There are people who insist they have been labeled "slow," "uneducated," "ghetto," and other derogatory terms for no other reason than the way they sound. How often do you label someone as educated or uneducated, professional or unprofessional, because of the way they sound?

The interesting factor behind paralanguage is that it is something that can be adjusted if desired. There are many who decide to take instruction in accent reduction or voice and diction in order to bring their patterns of speaking more in line with the dominant culture. Some feel this is necessary in the pervasive climate of competition. However, I advise individuals to be careful concerning their choices to lose their native tongues or purposefully become less ethnically identifiable. Language is where we find our identity. When we lose our language by choice or force, we lose a very important means of connecting to who we are. This is an interesting phenomenon in the United States. Europeans who settled the colonies of North America came from a myriad of European nations: I mean the Swiss, Germans, Irish, Dutch, Norwegians, French, and so on. Many, during their arrival at Ellis Island, changed their names and immediately began the process of losing their languages and accents of birth. Many purposefully did not hand down their ancestral languages to their children or their children's children, many for fear of ostracism. As a result, we have a major portion of Euro-Americans who have no connection to their historical languages. Some do not see themselves as ethnic; everyone else is *ethnic*. Yet there are hundreds of ethnic Euro dialects maintained by older generations and revitalized by a young generation throughout the Americas trying to hold on to its heritage.

Take another co-culture in the United States. The majority of African-Americans are the descendants of African slaves. During the centuries of slavery, Blacks were forbidden to speak their native tongues. In addition, they were not allowed to read or write English. Not only were they disconnected from their heritage/identity, they had to adopt a language that was not designed to express their personal experience in a favorable light. Blacks created pidgin dialects to survive and to try to re-create the cultural connections they had lost. Today most African-Americans still do not speak an African language or know where they are descended from. They have, however, always contributed abundantly to the evolving English lexicon and

American patterns of speaking. Many African-Americans speak what has been termed Ebonics, *Ebony Phonics*. There is still controversy as to whether this is a language or a dialect. I tend to refer to it as a dialect, much like Yiddish, Patois, or Spanglish. I use Ebonics comfortably and proudly within the settings where I feel it is appropriate to do so. These are primarily my home and social settings. I have also mastered General American English for the purposes of professional survival. I understand those who do and those who do not wish to operate bidialectically: again, communication is appropriate or inappropriate, not good or bad. I have several colleagues who have experienced what they consider workplace discrimination due to their unique cultural vocal patterns, whether it's speaking too loud, too soft, too slow, with a heavy accent, or in patterns riddled with cultural markers.

Our regional accents, dialects, and unique vocal patterns are what add the spice of diversity as we encounter each other within the myriad of communication settings where we find ourselves. The above examples focus on a prevalent concern in a work environment where conformity is ultimately rewarded over true individualism and without regard to the equality we espouse in our beliefs. It becomes too easy for some to forget that their origins are not of this land, a forgetfulness that can lead to feelings of ownership and ethnocentrism. For others, who have endured the identity crises of the absence of cultural and historical language, feelings of isolation and devaluation have become generational. *Language equals social reality.*

Determine for yourself whether your patterns of speaking are advancing your professional goals. Realize that symbols, verbal and nonverbal, create the organizational *reality* you are operating within. Your vocalics, or paralanguage, is a part of the message system others respond to every time you speak. You can change your pitch, tone of voice, rate, pacing, or any number of paralanguage qualities. However, your paralanguage is the unique personal identifier that distinguishes your voice from others. How often at work do we describe someone by saying, "You know the one that sounds like _____." We use paralanguage (vocalics) as a key identifier when describing others and when judging them. We categorize, label, and stratify others based on the way *they* speak. But we must wisely consider that accents, dialects, silence, cultural utterances, pitch . . . all these are the adornments of the verbal message. Paralanguage is to words as mind is to brain. It is the essence of our words.

ACTIONS DO SPEAK LOUDER THAN WORDS!

Our next nonverbal code, *kinesics,* is *the movement of the body in relation to sending and receiving messages.* It includes gestures, stance, posture, walk, eye contact, facial expression, and all other body movement engaged in relaying messages. When talking with colleagues, do you talk excessively with your hands? Avert your eyes when speaking to the boss or being spoken to? Walk down the hall with an easy saunter or a lively step? Do you stand erect or tend to lean on one hip? All of these body motions convey a message to others about you. Remember our definition: *communication is experienced whenever meaning is attributed to current behavior or past behavior.*

People differ in their use of body language; some tend to be more physically animated than others. This is often a cultural and/or family trait. It is important to understand that during our enculturation process as children, we learn thousands of nonverbal symbols that convey a variety of messages through the body. This is how we distinguish a frown from a smile, a wave hello from a wave goodbye, a look of approval from a look of dismay. I grew up with a mother who only had to give you that *look,* the one that immediately put you in your place. Eye contact as a variable of kinesics is one of the most powerful tools used to convey messages within every culture. With it we convey power, confidence, fear, love, and the list goes on. In the United States, eye contact is a primary determinant of the impression an individual gives of believability and trust. I have observed many lessen their chances for success during the process of interviewing because their eye contact did not convey a message of confidence, honesty, and self-assurance.

There are cultures where subordinates are not allowed to look directly in the eye those with sanctioned authority or of superior position. However, ours is not such a culture, and it is imperative that, in this highly competitive society, we understand the power of conveying assertiveness through our nonverbal communication. Check out your posture, your stance, and the face you wear when you think no one is looking. How engaged is your facial expression when you're in a meeting or speaking one-on-one with colleagues? A "real" face-lift is one that conveys a message of openness, self-assurance, and assertive listening.

We listen mainly with our eyes.

Too many of us walk around looking as if we carry the weight of the world on our shoulders. As a result, we often repel the very opportunities that may open new doors and horizons, opportunities that are only capable of appearing when you are present and focused. What message does your body language convey? Are you open to receive all that can be yours? If you are not sure, ask someone at work you trust. Awareness is the first step toward empowering your kinesics communication (see Application 2.1).

Application 2.1 - Seeing Is Believing!

Observe yourself. Engage in self-monitoring. Do you look at people when they are speaking to you? Do you look away when speaking to others?

Watch your patterns of eye contact with supervisors, coworkers, customers, and/or employees.

Record three occurrences of your eye contact behavior in a workday, preferably with different groups. Recognize how you perceive your position with different individuals based on eye contact.

IT'S ABOUT TIME!

Our next NVC code, *chronemics,* is *the study of time as a nonverbal system.* Time, as we understand and have adapted to it, is a *relative* concept. The way it is segmented, treated, and observed is a societal construct determined by culture. Time orientation in cultures may be *past, present,* or *future.* Some cultures concern themselves with aspects of their past history to determine their present, and other cultures may operate mainly in the present or else concern themselves with the affairs of the future. Cultures' level of technological advancement versus a more agrarian level will affect how they observe time. As a highly technological, future-oriented culture, the United States is very time conscious. It is what we call *monochronic.* Time is segmented according to activity; "time is money." In *polychronic* societies, time is a more holistic construct determined by ties to your family, clan, community, and nature. If you are to be successful in a culture that values time according to activity, you must construct your life around the responsibility of being on time for the prescribed activities or else risk being labeled irresponsible and unproductive. We look at the code again in Chapter 7, but I want to share a cultural perspective about chronemics.

Several readers may remember the cultural phrase "C-P time" or "colored people's time." An individual would say, "Pick me up at eight, and I don't mean C-P time." We understood that to mean "late," probably thirty minutes or more. But the actual marker of Blacks being prone to lateness or disregarding time came as a result of polychronic people being forced into monochronic patterns of dealing with time. West Africans were introduced into European-American time patterns foreign to the Africans' construct of time and its use. Others would try to use the disjunction as an indicator of the "inherent" laziness of Blacks, as witnessed by caricatures of the early to mid-1900s that reinforced the stereotypes of slothfulness. As I studied the construct of time within a cultural context, I began to realize the import of this cultural *assignment* toward Africans and other collective cultures. It was about the perception of time and its relationship to the context of the group. For the Africans, time was something to be used, not be used by. The social constructs of time collided (as they sometimes still do) and different time constructs came into contact with one another; hence the construct of "C-P time." Another example might be a vacation in the Caribbean, where the popular phrase "No problem, man" gives a glimpse of that culture's time consciousness. Or a siesta in Spain in the middle of the afternoon. A better definition of C-P time would be "communal potential time."

In U.S. culture we use time to indicate an individual's level of importance. The doctor may keep us waiting, but we do not keep the doctor waiting. We arrive *fashionably late* when we want to be noticed. We, as a culture, are said to have more stress-related diseases than most cultures because we are always in a hurry and our diet and health reflect this hurriedness. Think about your lunch break and *fast* food. When we examine time as a factor in the workplace, immediately we are connecting dozens if not hundreds of instances where timing is critical. It's always critical; that's why we have *dead*lines! Again, this is another arena within the work environment that affects bottom-line costs. Too many individuals are experiencing chronic absenteeism due to stress around time consciousness and constraints. Many studies have revealed that employees perform much better in environments where they are functioning at a productive level but not a destructive level. Time schedules legislated and strictly managed create stress-filled workplaces. The environment itself offers few if any destressors. It's an environment of one deadline after another, and very little collective, informal time. Robert Kegan, author of *In Over Our Heads: The Mental Demands of Modern Life,* writes, "People grow best where they continuously experience an ingenious blend of support and challenge. The balance of support and challenge lends to vital engagement." That needed *support* usually involves creating a more user-friendly working environment.

Employers need to first take stock of their pool of human capital. Consider the varying perspectives about time that may be exhibited in the office experience. Individuals that experience high family involvement and other communal experiences will likely be very valuable working in teams and with long-term projects. Employers should consider "lunch breakouts" to gather small groups for department discussions under a nonthreatening, nonurgent time frame. Think about what type of scheduling needs to be considered and how far out to make sure the team can move with relative ease through the project (see Application 2.2).

Think about how time is dealt with in your professional and personal life. Whose race are you running, and going where? How do you see yourself in connection to time in the office, around your colleagues? Maybe we need very different constructs for how we handle time in our professional lives and in our social lives. I know I did! I now go to the movies to relax, not to be on time. I now call my friends to chat, not just check in. I maintain my high level of time consciousness at work, but I give myself more time to get the job done.

 It's time to realize that the only person you are competing with is yourself and it's never too late to start your personal race toward self-fulfillment.

Application 2.2 - Is Time on Your Side?

Circle the candid answer and rate yourself.

1. How often do you rush through lunch?
   Never   Sometimes   Always

2. How often do you find yourself rushing your colleague's conversation, even in your head?
   Never   Sometimes   Always

3. How often are you late to work or to a meeting?
   Never   Sometimes   Always

4. How often do you feel rushed to finish an assignment at work?
   Never   Sometimes   Always

5. How often are you distracted by other things you need to be doing?
   Never   Sometimes   Always

Score system: Never = 1 point   Sometimes = 3 points
                 Always = 5 points

Results:

   1–5: You have mastered your time.

   6–15: Continue to lower your blood pressure and cholesterol.

   16–25: Promptly admit yourself to the nearest ER.

KEEP YOUR DISTANCE!

Proxemics is *the study of space and spatial relationships as a non-verbal code.* It also includes our use of objects and artifacts. The concept of space, as with the other NVC arenas, is that it is culturally bound. We highly value space in the United States. We treat it as a commodity. It is used to establish privilege and prestige. It is used to establish boundaries of success and power. It is used to protect one group from another. We aspire to big homes, sprawling grounds, huge office space, luxurious SUVs, and the like. We tend to distinguish the importance of an individual based on how much space the person has acquired. When you enter the boss's office, or if you're the boss, notice how much size and comfort play a role in distinguishing the supervisor's space from others'. Our office settings are full of cues that size matters!

Within the organizational context, we determine our relationship with others based on the amount of space we keep between them and ourselves—intimate distances versus more professional or public distances. Too often we assume this is the same everywhere, but it is not. Societies that have a collective consciousness see space as something to be shared. I often have conversations with individuals about how they were *invaded* at a checkout counter or a bank line by some *person* who was too close to them. Or the office worker who time and time again complains about a coworker violating their space. Think about the distance that you keep from a close colleague versus a "superior." Think about the way conference rooms are arranged or meeting spaces are prearranged. We lock our office doors to keep others out of our private workspace. This is based solely on the cultural adaptation of how we use, distribute, and operate in space.

U.S. Spatial Distance Mores

Intimate Distance—1 to 12 inches—Those we reach out to and touch

Personal Distance—12 inches to 2 feet—Friends and close associates

Social Distance—2 feet to 4 feet—Colleagues, doctor, mail clerk, . . .

Public Distance —4 feet and beyond—The ones labeled as "untouchables"

Materialism is one of the most important values of U.S. culture; we spend a lifetime acquiring the *things* that in our society represent having "made it." All societies place a certain value on things within their environments, but obviously some more than others. Notice how we treat our office space. How personal is it to you? Do you have an office, a cubicle, a corner, no space? Observe your desk for a moment. Any artifacts? What are they? Look around at your colleague's work spaces. Do you develop an impression of them based on their space? I worked with a fellow teacher for years who shared an office in my quad. The office was filled to the brim with papers, books, student projects, and so on. It was so packed that the instructor never went in there to sit, just to gather what he needed. He never counseled students in his office. Interestingly enough, his outer appearance was also disheveled and a bit slothful. The office situation finally got so bad, he was sent a notice to clean up the place, maintain it, or go without! Remember, how we use our space says something about us. And the boss notices!

How secure or insecure we feel in our space determines how we live in our spaces. Michael Moore, for his Oscar-award-winning documentary *Bowling for Columbine,* paid a visit to some neighborhoods in Canada to see if what he had heard about Canadians not locking their doors is true. The film shows him opening the doors of several homes that were not locked. Interviewing Canadian citizens, he listens to several attest they did not feel the need to lock their doors. They felt safe. Moore was surprised by their cultural outlook and the striking difference between their culture and U.S. culture, which advocates locking our doors consistently. Fear?

Observing a group of college students during an extended stay in Europe, I was struck by their acute awareness of how space did not have the same meaning and value as it did for them back in the United States. They consistently marveled at the small cars, extremely efficient use of space, close proximity of buildings and homes. Many quickly surmised that maybe they did not need as much space as they thought they did, nor all the objects and artifacts they used to fill their spaces.

What is your assessment of space in your life? How do you establish relationships based on your approach to space within your home and other communication environments, such as work? What are the taboos you are operating with and may not even be aware of? Are you isolating members of your team, possibly because of your strict space constraints or your lack of understanding or respect for U.S. spatial mores? What is the value you place on the *things* in your life? As the global village continues to shrink and more and more of us experience daily contact with others, it is important that we are aware of humanity's variations in spatial awareness and usage. We must make a global assessment of how our unique concept of space may not be in the best interest of a world where physical and natural resources are steadily being depleted and some being brought to the brink of extinction. As you read this book, what is the latest discussion on global warming and how is it affecting the way you live? Obviously, the concept of space and how we view and use it are very dire issues within the global community and impact every aspect of human existence.

The organizational space is a critical component to the flow and ease by which communication circulates through an environment. Is the meeting space comfortable, hygienic, and aesthetically pleasing? Do its colors stimulate thought and creativity? What type of meet-and-greet spaces does the organization promote for camaraderie and trust stimulation? Organizational space and spatial relationships silently operate to encourage the flow of communication or to stifle the flow. Which effect does your institution promote? (see Application 2.3).

SOMETIMES WHEN WE TOUCH

Haptics is the nonverbal code of *touching and touching behaviors as experienced during human communication*. Cultures en-

48

Application 2.3 - It's About Spaces!

Take an inventory of the organizational space. Are you stimulated when you walk through? Are there informal gathering spaces?

In each space you visit, make a comment about what works and what could work better.

Think outside of the box.

gage in a variety of touching rituals that reinforce the established do's and don'ts of public and private touching. Generally, most cultures have some taboos concerning touching that is invasive, violent, or perceived as *unnatural.* Within the context of U.S. culture, public displays of touching are not as taboo as they used to be, say, during the Puritan age. However, we do have established societal rules for public display, and we try to stay out of the privacy issues of a home unless there are issues of endangerment, such as with abused children.

In the workplace, we have the same or modified codes of appropriate touching, though often a bit more stringent due to concerns over harassment and diversity issues. The United States is known throughout the global marketplace for taking an informal perspective on touching in the work environment and relationships. The occasional pat on the back is permissible. Handshakes should be firm with meaning. An occasional peck on the cheek between some coworkers is OK. Some members in the workplace may be considered too aloof and others too "touchy-feely." How do you relate to touch in your intimate, social, or professional communication environments? How do your children, friends, colleagues view your approachability? Do you cringe when others try to give you a friendly embrace? How is your handshake: weak or limp, strong or clammy? (Remember Richard's fish handshake for Jill?)

Overall societal touching mores reveal the United States is pretty much in the middle of the road. We engage in more public touching than the Japanese, but not as much as Italians. We have a variety of greeting rituals that include formal hand-shaking, hugging, kissing on the cheek, backslapping, elaborate posturing, and so on. These rituals are grounded in our predominantly Judeo-Christian, patriarchal, and heterosexual culture. What is inappropriate for men is often seen as appropriate for women, and vice versa. Such clear demarcations have added to the complexity of gender relationships within the culture.

All of these responses to human touch are a matter of conditioning, but they can make or break our work relationships as we interact with diverse others in a culture full of ever-changing and ever-broadening experiences of human contact. This is why understanding sexual harassment in the workplace continues to be an area of concern due to the ever-broadening relationships men and women share, especially women from cultures outside the dominant U.S. culture.

Organizations should consider the gender and cultural makeup of the workplace environment in an effort to understand what types of touching mores may be present. These attitudes need to be taken into consideration and possibly attended to during orientation sessions that focus on workplace cultural dynamics. Organizational norms concerning appropriate and inappropriate touching should be established, not only as a sexual harassment issue but also a diversity concern.

DO YOU SMELL SOMETHING?

The last code we will examine in this section is *olfactory,* or *the study of smell as a nonverbal code.* Smell is often deemed the most memory-triggering sense of all five senses. We have strong attachments to what we consider good smells, powerful reactions against those we consider bad. This fact affects the way we live, eat, and interact with one another. How many times have your senses been assaulted by something you did not think smelled good? In the United States, we have a strong sense of what we consider to be pleasant smelling. Often, to those outside U.S. culture, we appear to be very *sterilized*. We shrink-wrap our foods, put our refuse far away from us, and utilize a variety of products to mask personal and societal odors we consider unpleasant.

Take body odor, for instance. Many societies feel more comfortable with natural body odors, enjoy the pungent smells of foods and spices that come through their pores, as well as have a different concept of what is clean, one different than the need to be odorless. I have advised some individuals new to our culture to buy new wardrobes or engage in the practice of using antiperspirants to deal with issues of body odor, not because they were not clean but because they did not "smell" the way we are used to. I have also had to advise travelers to adjust their sense of smell for the unfamiliar and often pungent odors they may not be used to. Again, as our global communities get closer and closer, we will all need to make adjustments in our levels of comfort, adjustments based on more heterogeneous paradigms of nonverbal behavior, including smell.

The workplace is no stranger to this situation, and there have been many instances where colleagues were uncomfortable with a smell belonging to a coworker, whether because of perfume or hygiene. There are times when people turn their noises up at an unfamiliar food with an equally unfamiliar smell. We all need to be a bit more respectful and adventurous in these cross-cultural experiences, or at least considerate.

You can see how the Nonverbal Communication symbols and messages embedded within the fabric of a culture are often the defining attitudes of how we interact with one another. NVC takes us underneath the surface of people's likes and dislikes, preferences and prejudices, the attitudes that so greatly affect their outlook and interaction with others. It is not *what* we say but *how* we say it that establishes our work relationships. Empower your communication environments with the knowledge of these basic but powerful nonverbal communication concepts. Create a better understanding between yourself and the people you interact with nonverbally every day. Use your nonverbal communication as a means of supplementing your verbal messages so that they are congruent; avoid being labeled a walking contradiction. Use NVC to empower your interviews, evaluations, department meetings, and public and impromptu speaking opportunities. Your awareness and manipulation of the NVC arenas of step two offer a whole new focus in repairing and enriching the organizational environment.

You have journeyed from step one to step two: understanding the connection between your self-image and your self-expression through nonverbal language. As you now move yourself into the mental, emotional, and physical space of others, you take *you* with you. We watched Jill move through her day with her Intrapersonal and Nonverbal communication into each and every communication event she experienced at work. The Communication Staircase offers insight into the interconnectedness of all your communication experiences, starting with you!

Q & A Nonverbal Communication

Dear PS,

Q: One of my coworkers talks really loud! So loud it gets in the way of focusing on her message. She's a great worker though!

A: It's interesting and very true that our nonverbal message will always count more than our verbal message. This paralanguage difference can be a serious communication barrier. Culturally, we have a comfortable and acceptable decibel-level-of-volume etiquette. When anyone operates outside the acceptable levels, too loud or too soft, there is a level of discomfort. Tell her. Be sincere. Ask if she can tell that her volume is usually above normal levels. She may not know or may confide she cannot help it. Work out a signal with her to help her gauge.

Q: I have an employee who is habitually late to meetings. He is punctual for work, but meetings are a problem. And he always has a good excuse!

A: If he "always has a good excuse," I would ask myself, as the initiator of these meetings, is he the only person lagging? Are other members overstretched? Are you "meeting" your people to death? Is the problem a time cultural barrier that has not been addressed? First, examine the meeting culture of your organization. Depending on your analysis, you may need to approach the late member and stress meeting etiquette or enroll him in a time-management workshop. You can also choose to have "stress free" gatherings that combine lunch, recreation, or coffee chats with agendas that are not too pressuring.

Q: I really do not appreciate the way my colleague keeps his desk area. It's really messy and I am embarrassed to bring clients into the area.

A: Since your area mate may not be the only one in the department suffering from "messyitis," I would suggest that human resources or the facilities department send out a notice in the newsletter or an interoffice memo requiring a certain standard of workspace image. Stress the client contact with the work area and the importance of image. You can also stick a note on his desk saying CLEAN THIS CRAP UP! Just do not sign my name.

Q: I am uncomfortable with how one of my colleagues consistently invades my space! No matter how much I back up, she keeps closing in! I think she is Hispanic, so I do not know if this is a cultural thing.

A: You are right that not everyone has the same personal space requirements, and ours in the United States tend to be very guarded. And yes, it may be cultural in terms of the awareness of U.S. personal boundaries. If your company is diverse, especially if it includes first- and second-generation immigrants, your orientation programs should include a communication component that introduces the employee to Nonverbal Communication in the workplace. Please be a good coworker and let her read the material about nonverbal issues and culture in this chapter and Chapter 7. You will improve her chances of success!

Q: I have a member of my team who wears clothing I think is a bit informal for the workplace. It's more like something a young woman would wear to a club. I am a male supervisor and I find the topic a bit sensitive to broach. Any ideas?

A: Yes! Engage a mature, tactful senior female member of her department and talk with the senior member privately about your concerns. If she concurs, then ask her to facilitate the young lady's awareness. I would suggest the three of you meet. After you have introduced the need for a "work-related observation," you leave the room and let the female member talk with her and advise her of more appropriate choices. You can request that they both contact you afterward for further clarification if necessary. You can also call HR and ask that they approach the worker. But you are right to seek support. Also, don't forget to tell her about the areas she is doing well in.

Interpersonal Communication

You can fool some of the people all of the time, and all of the people some of the time, but you can't fool all of the people all of the time.

—Abraham Lincoln

FIVE KEYS TO POSITIVE, HEALTHY WORK RELATIONSHIPS

The third step you are about to ascend will make for one of the most in-depth chapters you will read in this guide. Interpersonal Communication is truly a science of human investigation, awareness, and adaptation. Factors of socialization, perception, and diversity can make interpersonal communication a complex experience in the workplace. However, there are skills and ingredients you can use to move your communication ability forward. These skills can best be introduced within five (5) vital keys to successful interpersonal relationships.

55

Key #1

Be the Person YOU Want to Work With!

Being a confident, whole person is about living purposefully, aware of personal responsibility, self-determination, and active participation. That *right person* is the one we come in touch with through the self-reflection and self-monitoring found in step one, our Intrapersonal Communication. Understanding the role of your self-talk, you are now acutely aware of how Nonverbal Communication greatly impacts your message. Not only are you aware of the 93 percent that NVC can potentially play in your sending and receiving a message, you now have a working knowledge of the vastness of the nonverbal experience, from time to touching.

The individual whose self-esteem and self-worth are balanced achieves professional satisfaction. Life is not about seeking outward approval but experiencing inward approval by thinking right thoughts, speaking right words, and creating right actions about your career and aspirations. You must determine for yourself the level of professional success you want. Your thoughts, emotions, and words should affirm this goal.

It is during and because of the journey of self-discovery that we touch others. We get to know ourselves through others, even at work. The experiences of life come in the form of connecting with others. We need and desire companionship and self-affirmation to support us through the journey of life. We create experiences to interact with each other and create society. These experiences create the interpersonal relationships in our lives. Your Intrapersonal Communication meets you right at the door of your Interpersonal Communication experiences. *You* take *you* wherever *you* go. During steps one and two, we focused on understanding more about the self and personal perception; now we will focus on self in connection with others, namely coworkers.

We have examined the process of personal communication behaviors that affect your self-esteem, perceptions, and personal beliefs. These are the internal processes of communication that manifest in your interactions with others. It all begins within you and expands like the ripple on the water, affecting the quality of relationships in your life—your lake. In this third step, we want to examine your relationship to the *cast members* in your movie called Work.

Interpersonal Communication can be defined as a *dyadic exchange where at least one person is attributing meaning to the other's behavior,* or as *the exchange of messages between two people.* How do we come together in our interpersonal exchanges? What are the rules of engagement? One of the most important keys to understanding relationships can be found in the *Law of Attraction.* This immutable universal law has existed since the beginning of time and basically states that "like attracts like." Negative energy attracts negative, and positive energy attracts positive. In layman terms, you cannot have a peaceful and satisfying work experience if you are not peace filled and satisfied. You are attracting to yourself circumstances AND people according to the *communication* signals you put forth. This includes your experiences at work and relationships with coworkers. As we grow into adults, very few of us are given a formula of how to seek out and create relationships that work. Often our relationships are nothing more than the search for personal validation: "Someone see me as I see myself and validate for me that I am OK." This need for self-validation often creates superficial bonds with other individuals having the same need for self-approval.

Remember the game of *Pac-Man?* The little Pac-Man figure races through the *game of life* trying to see how many other entities he can eat up. Depending on how much he can devour, he wins the game. Relationships at work are often played out like little Pac-Men gobbling one another up. Competition, greed, and self-absorption in the workplace fuel the Pac-Man syndrome.

Too often these relationships boil down to "what can you do for me?" We must be aware of the intent involved in our relationships. Too often we form relationships based on how they benefit us. This is especially true in the workplace, where everyone just wants to get ahead. We often walk around with a "You give, I get" philosophy and quickly disregard those we feel provide no benefit. Realizing as much gives insight into communication conflict within the organization. Beware of *talking* to others, versus *communicating* with others. Sometimes we talk just long enough to get what we want or need for the job or goal. We "gobble up" each others' value, ideas, and suggestions in the effort to advance our own missions. Recognize the Pac- Man syndrome in you.

Next, there is the need to understand the role of how we form relationships with others. Our relationships are mainly reflections of ourselves. Others transmit to us through **mirror messages,** the *messages we receive from others that are a direct reflection of how we see ourselves*. Our thoughts, our words attract others of like energy. Remember the Law of Attraction? Everyone looks for that mirror image to validate the self, positive or negative (see Figure 3.1).

I remember one of my first introductions to this concept in action. I went to my first Broadway play well over 25 years ago. The name of the play and its performers escape me now, but not the dramatic dilemma. There was a young woman *in* love with what we would term a gigolo. She worked several jobs to keep him living in the style he had become accustomed to: fancy cars, nice suits, expensive liquor, and money in his pockets. She was virtually a prisoner in the home she paid for, except when working. She cooked, cleaned, and made herself available to him when he wanted her. At other times, she would pine away for him while he ran the streets, drinking and carousing with other women. When he stayed out all night, she was forbidden to question him for fear of physical retaliation. I sat through the play wondering why she would allow herself to

© PS Perkins

Figure 3.1 Mirror Messages

be so taken advantage of, grimacing during every verbal and physical assault.

As the play climaxed, and the *happy ending* approached, she finally came to her senses and decided to leave one night while he was out. She left with nothing but the clothes on her back. As the play started to fast-forward, she finally decided to pursue the dreams of her youth and go back to school, eventually graduating from law school, passing the bar, and becoming a partner at a prestigious law firm. One day, when entering her downtown office building, she almost tripped over a man in the lobby cleaning floors. You guessed it. It was her *ex-pimp*. At the moment of recognition, there was an awkward silence, then the usual questions of "How you doing?" She related that she went back to school and became a partner with a successful law firm housed in the top floor of the building in whose lobby he was standing. He sheepishly acknowledged he always knew "she would be somebody." They mumble their awkward good-byes. But just as she was about to walk away, she turned around to confront him. "I have waited 10 years to be able to ask you, why when I loved you the way that I did, giving you my all, being everything I could for you, why, why did you treat me like a doormat?" He looked down at the floor, scratching his head, and then slowly but definitively replied, "Because you let me." Curtain down.

People generally act as a mirror by treating you the way they perceive you treat yourself.

I got it right away, and it is a lesson I have thought about many times throughout my life and the myriad of relationships I have experienced. Let's reread that important key to interpersonal relationships. *People generally treat you as you treat yourself.* What do these mirror messages tell you about yourself as you come in contact with them daily? Apply this to both your work and social relationships. This can be especially true for the work environment, where individuals are taking less time than in personal and social settings to "get to know you" and will more likely take the external and internal cues you give off, just as a time-saver. We often resent this manner of surface interaction when we are the recipient of it, but often do not recognize this tendency in our own selves. So it is more imperative in the work setting that we make sure to take the time to value individuals at work by learning to *be* the person you want to work with! If you are OK with yourself, others are OK with you! You do not need to scapegoat others when you have worked through your own issues. All of our lakes are full of the mirror messages we have received from others that have created the image we have of ourselves until we create our own image. *Be* the right person for your individual self and you will establish relationships at work that reflect the respect, inclusion, and collaboration necessary to a positive work experience.

Key #2

Choose the Right People—Make the Right Connections

It is not easy to foster work relationships built on trust and mutual support. But you are off to a great start when you realize personal responsibility is the first quotient in the equation. We need to be prepared for the work that goes into making relationships substantive and building teams that are high functioning. Too often we live in our *expectations* of how a coworker should be. We place people in our little *expectation boxes* and expect them to stay. You have a box for your teammate, your boss, your employee. We even sometimes codify the boxes into rules that everyone must adhere to. We all carry these expectations with us throughout our workday. When we do not get the results, response, or support we expect, we blame others for getting out of their boxes. We must mature beyond the prescribed boxes we create for others just because we are too lazy, disenchanted, or distracted to experience other people from their reality. Resorting to our boxes, treating people according to the preconceived notions we have of them, can hamper all processes of communication including listening, empathy, and flexibility. You will discover that when you let others out of the box, you can also get out of the box you have made for yourself.

This is where we make the connections that bring us satisfaction in our professional experiences. You meet people where they are and determine, without judgment, how the relationship can be fostered as a win-win relationship of mutual teamwork and support. Avoid Pac-Man. With every person you encounter, there is the need to suspend judgment and allow room for their reality to shine through. We must seek to communicate in a way that values differing perspectives and ways to achieve the organizational goal.

We need to undersand that effective communication, though not a panacea, is the cure to most of what ails human relationships.

We need to engage in the much-needed process of authentic *self-disclosure*. Self-disclosure is *what we share with others.* We wear masks at work so we can be impenetrable or portray a certain image. We need to elevate our close associates to a level of individuality. Interpersonal communication is an art and it is a science of rules greatly affected by perspective.

Let's examine more critically our *life movie.* Don't you just love a good movie? We support the movie industry, one that brings many endless hours of distraction from the everyday realities we are living. Movies offer a vicarious opportunity to live the experiences of the imagined other. For many it is a ritual of escape. Escape from what? Your own movie! Are you starring in your movie? Have you ever felt like your life in its various phases feels like a drama being played out? Well, to a large extent, it is! Shakespeare once said, "All the world's a stage, and all the men and women merely players." We are all playing out our major role in the movie of life.

Now the question is, "Who wrote your *life movie script* and how is it being directed?" Take for instance the drama you play out at work every day. What role(s) do you play at work and who have you assigned your movie rights?

Featuring Your Life Movie

Star—This should be YOU—the person who gives life to the mental script based on their *own* thoughts, words, and deeds.

Producer—The individual(s) who control(s) the *purse strings* of your life; maybe your boss who gets to determine who will be allowed to play, at what level, and with what results.

Director—The person or people who control the specific action of the script, who tell you how to play your role in life—the people you have given control of your script.

Scriptwriter—The voice that produces the words that create your movie—YOUR LIFE. Whose words are controlling you? How do your words in the workplace affect your relationships? (Remember the platter.)

Costars—The individuals most central to the action of your life: parents, siblings, significant others, those you allow significant control over the script of your movie. Those we don't always choose to be a part of our movie but whom we do choose to maintain in our daily script. At work, these are the individuals most directly linked to your job performance.

Supporting Cast—The individuals we choose to have frequent interactions with: our peers, acquaintances, coworkers from a different department, individuals who make up the support systems of our lives and thus greatly influence our outlook on life.

Special Guest Appearances—People who just seem to keep popping up in the movie whether invited or not. At work, it's that person you experience at the monthly division meeting.

Cinematographer—Where are you, how did you get there, who is responsible for the way your life looks, who is capturing the pictures of your life? How far, how big, how little have you allowed yourself to dream? How have others influenced the vision of your movie? Who is designing the *portfolio* of your career?

Musical Composer—Who conducts the musical score of your life on a daily basis? At work are you a follower or a leader? When necessary are you a team player or a rebel? Whose beat are you listening to? Are you a part of the notes of harmony or the notes of discord in your work environment? Is your work experience half full or half empty?

Costumer—Who is dressing you every day? What is that outer image you portray to the world; what is the nonverbal façade you present each day? And is it a true image of the real you, or are you just trying to fit in?

Technical Experts—The people behind the scenes, the ones handling the *lights,* the *camera,* the *sound boards,* the organization at large. We do not always look on them as affecting our movie, but they can play a significant role in how we see ourselves.

The *life movie* roles above should help you create a good sketch that allows you to understand the relationships you are fostering at work. So the question remains, who are the *cast members* and *crew* in your drama called Work? Who are the people playing the roles listed above? Do you star in the major responsibilities? Or have you given your creative power over to someone else? How are these interpersonal relationships adding to or subtracting from the quality of your work experience? These are the individuals who provide the majority of the mirror messages you receive every day at work, in addition to their personal work dramas. Many decide to fall in step with the countless others playing an *extra* in their own movies. Be honest with yourself. Are you having the adventure of your life? Is your job adding to or detracting from your desires to live your passion? It is important to note that no one is born or lives intending to live an average life. We start to settle for mediocrity, then forget how to dream, how to be open to the possibilities. We go to sleep. We give away our rights to produce our movie.

Have you ever felt that, if it were not for other people's problems, you wouldn't have any? Well, to a certain extent this may be true. Think about the multiple messages you receive every day from those you have invited into your work space. Depending on their placement in your workday, the messages of some will affect you more than the messages of others; say, for instance, your boss or colleague versus the mailroom clerk. Obviously, the *co-stars* impact your daily emotional, mental, and physical state more than an organizational member you interact with once a month.

It is the casts in our life movie that determine the quality of our relationships. We are too often concerned with *how many* people we connect with, versus *the quality* of connections. Often times we wear our emotional selves down trying to give the same energy and focus to everyone in our movie no matter what level of contribution they make to our total well-being. Take the stereotypical husband/father who puts in more hours at the office than he does at home and spends more quality time with the people he works with than his own children. As the years pass, he wonders why the kids never call and always seem to forget his birthday. Who are your co-stars? In Jill's movie, we see her interacting with her co-stars and supporting cast. What can we learn from these roles and their individual impact on the *star's* (your) *movie* (life)?

We are each given an empty screen at birth. We each create a script with our thoughts and words. The empty screen given to each of us at the beginning of life turns into the movie of our lives. We are ALL given the unique gift of creative power. To create what? Your life! This includes the types of relationships we want to foster with others. Here is where the plot comes in. The plot of the script is conceived in the writer's mind; then the screen comes to life with the experiences being played there. That *life movie script* is written on a daily basis and determines the outcome of each and every encounter and experience you have on a moment-to-moment basis within the communication environment.

This is the underlying thought behind personality-type tests. You cannot deal with others based on personality quotients. Yes, it is sometimes helpful to categorize tendencies, but this is not how you relate communicatively with people. You are not communicating with type A or type B. You are communicating with Juanita, who is angry about the work overload. We meet people where they are, and by listening effectively and making room for their perspective, we can connect with them and better understand how to work together.

A personal guru of positive thought once said to me, "Have a wonderful day; it's always your choice." I initially scoffed at her remark, challenging her about the daily circumstances of life that I did not feel I had a *choice* in. (It had been a particularly challenging day.) She gently guided me through the process of seeing my role in these experiences where my *victim consciousness* consistently took away my personal choice. She explained, "We do not always choose the circumstances that we encounter within every given moment of our lives; however, we always have a choice as to how we react to those encounters and thus regain control of the experience. In other words, it is the *way* you define it. How you label it is what it is—every experience. Have a wonderful day; it's always your choice." The resistance to this truth has plagued the human experience for millennia. We too often want to relish our victim consciousness and abdicate responsibility for our personal choices, including our responsibilities to the individuals we allow a role in our lives. So, back to our cast members at work. Who is it at work that irritates you to no end? Who makes you *feel* inferior? Think about the characters playing a role in your organizational movie and use the exercise below to identify these individuals. Individuals truly starring in their own movie will find that they are in control of the majority of the roles necessary to their daily and future script. How would you label your work relationships? Open? Respectful? Productive? Is it time for a few *pink slips?* In other words, getting rid of a few cast members who have not added positively to your script. Make the right connections with others at work by choosing to foster healthy relationships (see Application 3.1).

Application 3.1 - Who's in Your Movie?

Create a new movie and STAR in it! Start today by engaging in a simple but powerful exercise. Create your *life movie script.*

Make a list of the people you interact with at work on a daily basis, filling in the roles of the movie analogy.

Once you create your list, examine your relationship with these individuals and their impact on your life. Is it time to change your characters? Are you starring in your own movie?

Key #3

Make Room for the Other Person's Reality

There are numerous hypotheses and theories about the rules that govern human interaction. I will even venture as far as to say that there are absolutes in the realm of human interaction. One such absolute states that when communication transpires, it is always a complete process. It happens whenever meaning is attributed to behavior. The duration or outcome of the exchange does not matter, only that it did transpire and there was awareness on at least one participant's part. How is this so? Most are not aware that there are at least seven basic ingredients to the dyadic interpersonal exchange. Each of these ingredients plays a major role in determining the success of the communication exchange. All seven are present in every communication experience. The working knowledge of these ingredients allows the communication environment to be influenced and controlled for maximum benefit. Whenever there is communication, these ingredients are present and working to ensure either the success or failure of the exchange. They exist and work together, one feeding off of the other. Consider the basic Dyadic Communication Model in Figure 3.2.

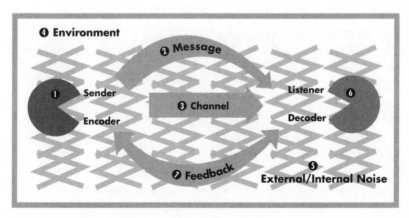

Figure 3.2 Ingredients of Dyadic Communication

Seven Basic Ingredients of Every Communication Experience

The sender, or the encoder, creates or encodes the message for the intended receiver. As sender, you are responsible for making sure that your message is created and received in the manner intended. Think about the importance of how a message is delivered. You must take into consideration both the verbal and nonverbal nuances of the message as you contemplate whom the message is being encoded for. Which brings us to another communication absolute: the content of a message and the relationship that you have with its receiver are inextricably tied together. You always create a message with someone in mind, even if that someone is you. You must create a message that is digestible to the intended receiver. The quality of the message, its ability to be understood, is very dependent upon your ability to exercise your communication power in relation to the reality of the other person. Remember *mirror messages*. It all begins with you and the quality of your movie!

The message you create is developed out of the resources of your mind, which include your memories, vocabulary, associations, likes/dislikes, needs, wants, desires, and so on. Your perception shapes your messages based on how you see the world. No two people are alike. When interpreting a message from you, they will draw on a totally different pool of resources and may or may not draw the desired conclusion you are hoping for. However, if you take this into consideration during the encoding process, you stand a chance of being understood. Since no two people are alike, every time you encode a message for a different individual, you must critically contemplate a new set of possible outcomes. Many have yet to find the voice within that they are comfortable with. Too many rely on others to read their minds because they do not have the ability to say what needs to be said, often relying on their nonverbal message system (which step two reveals can often be misinterpreted). There are always two messages—the one you send and the one they receive. How many times have your messages been misunderstood by a coworker or you misunderstood a coworker's intentions? Nonverbal messaging considerably adds to the possibility of communication barriers. Communicating effectively requires critical thinking and listening skills, as well as the ability to express your ideas in a variety of situations.

An important aspect of being involved in a communication experience is your ability to contribute. Have something to say! Many people do not feel comfortable fully engaging others in meaningful conversation—"meaningful" being determined by the level of self-disclosure involved. Do not be afraid to participate, contribute, and ask questions. Read more! Increase your vocabulary. Stay informed about community and world events. Messages are created out of your personal, professional, and global repertoire. Do you have one? Are you aware of what is going on in the company, through formal and informal networks? Are you aware of the latest news affecting industry trends? Are you a good communicator in one-to-one exchanges or group meetings? How about the communication of conflict? Do you have the interpersonal skills all organizational environments thrive on? Follow the tips given in this section.

The channel is the instrument through which communication flows. There are a variety of communication channels, and technology offers more and more each day. The channel affects the way that the message is received. Think about how you respond to a phone call versus a letter versus face-to-face communication. Very few of us take the time to consider the impact the channel has on the reception of our messages. However, we often respond vehemently when we receive a message in a manner we deem inappropriate. It only takes a few seconds to make an adjustment before we dial that number or click that send button. Stop and think! The right channel could be the decisive factor. Ever receive an inappropriate e-mail at work? Ever witness a coworker say something in public that was inappropriate? Ever leave a note or mail a letter that you could not retrieve? Stop and take a moment to choose the most effective channel.

The fourth ingredient is situation or context. All communication takes place within a context. This includes time, place, and circumstance. Again, the effective communicator must rely on critical thinking processes to assess whether, for the best possible outcome, the encoded message should be delivered in a particular setting. We have all heard of the proverbial "foot in mouth" syndrome. Too often people don't take the time to determine whether they should delay sending a message in a particular fashion at a particular time. We see this scenario played out in the office setting time and time again. We have all witnessed an exchange that was poorly timed and thus poorly received. Then there are others who miss the opportune time altogether because they cannot find their voice—they are governed by fear of rejection. Think of the impact this has on professional relationships, employment, and other business and social exchanges. Timing *is* everything.

 Think about a time you chose one channel over another. Why e-mail instead of face to face or a text instead of a voice call?

Interference, or noise, is the fifth ingredient. Within every communication exchange, we experience a certain degree of noise that can interfere with the clarity of the message. It is important that the sender consider the level of noise that may be present during the exchange, in order to minimize its impact. This noise takes place on two levels for both the sender and the receiver. It is both *internal* and *external*—inside the mind and also outside, part of the environment. The sender has some control over the external noise. He can choose to turn off the television, put the kids to bed, or request that the receiver stop reading the paper. He can even forgo an exchange, say no to trying to communicate in a busy restaurant or while the kids are running around screaming. He can also control the noise inside his head, the thoughts that pervade his mind, while trying to get his point across. We all experience this. We can think much faster than we can talk. Many times we are on to our next point mentally before we even conclude the statement we are making. Or we may be second-guessing how the receiver is going to reply. What is most difficult to control is the internal noise within the listener. It is up to the encoder to make sure that the message relayed is clear enough, mutually beneficial enough, and interesting enough for the listener to *turn down the volume* in their minds long enough to get the full intent of the sender's message. Since no two people are alike and quite possibly they may have different objectives concerning the communication exchange, being able to quiet internal noise is often the most crucial factor within the communication environment. Remember, the majority of noises, the major distractions, are often nonverbal in nature. Keep your eyes and mind involved in the communication experience.

Now we turn our attention to the receiver/decoder/listener. In order to ensure a positive outcome, all ingredients previously discussed must be assessed before bringing in the receiver. These ingredients exist with or without your knowledge. They always have, they always will. It is up to the effective communicator to use them to his benefit. Now that you have thoughtfully encoded your message, chosen the most effective channel, considered the most appropriate setting, and rid your environment of all distracting noises, you stand a better chance of getting your message across in the manner you wish it to be received by the listener. The key here is to make room for the listener's reality. This is something that is very hard for most I-N-D-I-V-I-D-U-A-L-S to do. We are so busy seeing everything from our personal points of view that we create messages with only ourselves in mind, to satisfy ourselves, and then we can't figure out why others just can't get it! Effective communication in the workplace is a process of sharing not just words but realities. This is the reason that self-disclosure is so important to working relationships. You need to know the individual so that you can communicate in a manner that takes into consideration their perspective. This takes time.

The last ingredient in this list of basics is feedback. This relates to the cyclical responses shared between the communication participants. We receive feedback from our listeners through both verbal and nonverbal responses. Head nods, wrinkled foreheads, eye contact, vocal responses, and the like. Too often we are so busy trying to get our point across, we ignore the messages that are coming to us loud and clear! Feedback allows us to do a very important thing during the communication exchange: *adjust!* It tells us to stop, keep going, clarify, or shut up! It gives us the much-needed cues to know whether or not our message is being received in a positive or negative manner. During the exchange, the process of feedback keeps the conversation going. The next time you are engaged in a discussion, examine the level of feedback you are receiving. You may be surprised at how much you let slip right by you (see Application 3.2).

These seven basic ingredients become more complex when you factor in the sociological, psychological, and physiological factors of the participants' backgrounds. Perception is the lens through which each individual sees life. It is highly personal and highly guarded. I remember a phrase from the classic comedy series *Good Times*. The father was challenging a teacher who ques-

Application 3.2 - 7 Ingredients of Communication

During your next planned meeting with a coworker or a group meeting, record the seven ingredients of the communication experience.

Who is the sender, the situation, noise, etc.? What was the outcome? Examine the seven ingredients. How did they perform to add to the effectiveness of the experience?

Make a habit of considering the ingredients of the communication experience BEFORE you exchange, then watch the positive change!

tioned his son's IQ because he could not answer test questions that were framed from a Eurocentric perspective. James retorted, "How you gon' understand where I'm coming from if you ain't been where I been? You dig?" It is all about perspective. We can only come to one another from where we come. When we go to work, we take us with us. We engage others from the core of our belief system. You should be gaining insight into why harmonious communication is sometimes so hard to achieve. Something as simple as the choice of how to send out a department message or what refreshments should be at the office meeting? Everyone wants it their way. The ability to positively manipulate the ingredients of the basic communication model helps create a communication climate that fosters understanding. Some may say, "I don't have time to think about all this stuff every time I get ready to talk to someone!" You really don't have time not to! And it only takes a moment, a split second to make some of the decisions necessary to determine whether you should or should not open your mouth! The message is sensitive—*don't send an e-mail.* The room is crowded—*don't bring up the problem.* There are too many distractions—*wait until you are alone!* These are simple remedies to help avoid what can turn out to be very complex, destructive patterns within relationships. Try the exercise in Application 3.3.

Recognize the ability to manipulate your communication setting and influence your outcomes! Play a stronger, more strategic role in the outcome of your communication experience. You will start to recognize how your life is being positively influenced by your taking control of your communication environment. It works.

INTERPERSONAL CONFLICT

It is important to understand that conflict is normal and that it can be highly productive when experienced between two individuals who have the mutual aim of trying to understand one

Application 3.3 - Miscommunication Tools

Think of the last discussion you had with a coworker or friend that did not produce the type of results you were hoping for.

Now go over the seven ingredients we just discussed. Could one or more of these ingredients have played a role in the miscommunication? Could you or the other participant have handled one or more components a little differently? Chosen a different place and time? Encoded a different message?

Go over each ingredient and see how easy and beneficial it is to think before you speak!

another and move the company's bottom line forward. But, of course, it does take two. You are only responsible for yourself. You lead by example. Remember when our parents used to say, "Do as I say and not as I do!" Well, we did not buy it then, and those you interact with are not buying it now. Effective communication starts within and by applying some simple, common-sense principles such as those detailed in this guide. Start by examining your communication environments at work and with close friends. What is the quality of your communication *climate?* What are the mirror messages you send and receive? How often do your expectations get in the way of reality? Is it time to take off the *rose-colored glasses?* We need to engage in communication that is supportive. By "supportive," I mean respectful and open to the other's reality. We need to be more aware of the caustic communication that leads to destruction and pain, first of all within ourselves. Some of us have spent a lifetime sharing pain with others, like bottom-feeders in a lake. We have become addicted to negativity. We bring this energy into the workplace with us. We have alienated ourselves from understanding that happiness is the journey and not just the destination. Our relationships are fulfilled in the experience of the moment, not in the imagined or the hoped for. That is one of the reasons carefully choosing your cast is so important. Are you sure you are in the right environment to nurture your genius so that you can get about the business of experiencing life abundantly and harmoniously? Too many of us have "settled" for mediocre jobs, relationships, and experiences and spend a lifetime blaming others. It is never too late to recover what is important to you. Is this your dream career? Are you building your career in the right environment with the right people? Much of the conflict within the organizational environment stems from people who are unhappy with themselves and their choices. It is vital that the organization help to create and maintain a communication climate that encourages interpersonal relationships that are supportive and productive.

SUPPORTIVE VERSUS DEFENSIVE COMMUNICATION

Your communication at work can be just as sensitive as your communication in your personal life. We all want to feel valued and respected. There are many areas of corporate communications that require skill and tact to maintain a communication climate that is positive and thriving. How do you add to the communication climate? How would others describe your ability to handle and resolve conflict at work? Since we understand that conflict is normal, the question becomes how we handle conflict. As discussed above, the first area of attention is within yourself and the awareness of how much your ego plays a role in creating conflict. Typical styles of conflict resolution include:

Passive → Aggressive

Neutral → Detached

Avoidance → Unresolved

Assertive → Aggressive

Most of the above patterns are based on the individual's upbringing and how the person has been taught to handle the stress associated with conflict. Oftentimes the interpersonal dynamic is complicated by differing cultural perspectives on the value and manner in which conflict is addressed. The Euro-American pattern has traditionally been seen as passive-aggressive. This can oftentimes be at odds with co-cultures in the workplace that use a more assertive-aggressive approach, such as African-Americans, or what may appear to be the neutral, detached approaches of some Asian cultures. With so many varying patterns, it can be difficult to determine how to best conduct conflict-management solutions. Understanding that conflict is normal and can even be constructive, the best approach is to infuse into the communication climate skills that move individuals beyond their individual patterns. *Supportive Communication* versus *Defensive Communication* helps individuals to understand that communicating in a particular manner is more productive and will benefit the outcome they seek. Examples of the difference between the types of patterns:

Supportive Communication	Defensive Communication
Problem-centered	Blame-centered
Cooperative	Competitive
Uses descriptive "I"	Uses accusative "You"
Open to differing perspectives	Egotistical
Compassionate	Self-centered

Again, many conflicts are a matter of individuals trying to prove they are right and consistently seeking to confirm that rightness no matter what. This makes for a very unhealthy communication climate and encourages the Pac-Man syndrome introduced earlier. In order to avoid this syndrome, we need to concentrate on being whole circles, complete within ourselves, as discussed in Chapter 1. Otherwise, we may confuse our story for someone else's. The 2006 hit movie, *The Devil Wears Prada,* offered an interesting insight into the choices we make concerning our professional lives and the pressures to conform to certain definitions of success. The young heroine admired the fashion industry but was more interested in journalistic reporting. She took a job at a prestigious fashion magazine to gain exposure and skills, but this is where her confusion began. She began to be taken in by the trappings of glamour, beauty, and power. An interesting series of relationship experiences with her boss, coworkers, and friends inevitably convinced her that she made certain choices based on illusions she fed herself about a fictitious world, one she was not prepared to risk her happiness and peace of mind for. There were others who were more appropriately suited for that specific organizational environment. I appreciated the movie's insight to call attention to the pervasive problems of self-image and the way women feel compelled to hold themselves to unattainable measurements of prescribed beauty. Remember, who we are comes from deep within us and reaches out to touch all those around us. It is the *communication ripple.* As the movie progressed, the heroine began to *star in her own movie* and rebel against socially imposed definitions of success. She wrote a new life script. Are you ready for one?

You may have heard this saying: "People come into our lives for a reason . . . a season . . . or a lifetime." Too often we are so busy trying to make every relationship a lifetime or co-star experience instead of allowing the relationships to flow through the seasons and/or enrich the reasons of our lives. But, regardless of our insistence, this is usually how relationships develop. Not everyone is meant to work effortlessly with you or think you as bright as you know you are. How do we create meaningful, lasting, and healthy social and professional relationships? Again, back to step one. It all starts with you and self-love. It starts with the cleansing of your water, the healing of your mind, your emotional stability and health.

Once this is well into the process of realization and you are becoming a whole circle, you can then start to experience the most important key to a healthy relationship with someone else: making room for the other person's reality. This is the vital key to experiencing a shared, loving interpersonal relationship. Once you are safe and secure within the script you have written for your life, you can determine whether the other person's script is one you want to share in, without judgment and competition. You must be in tune with who you are so you know what you are attracting and how it fits into your life. If you do not know who you are and what you want, there are always thousands of people lined up to tell you who you are not and sell you what you do not want or need. This occurs in both our personal and professional lives.

Everyone is experiencing a different reality. It is very unwise to think that others see things exactly the way you do. But this is why we form groups and associations to mirror ourselves. However, within the most homogeneous groups there are distinct differences. You often marvel at how different you are from your siblings, who were raised in the same household with you. We make room for the other's reality, and this must be done every time we share communication with another person. Try to step into the perspective being shared, or at least allow the other person the right to have an opinion. This is especially important for problem-solving groups, decision-making groups, teams, couples, all those who must accept the consequences of a particular action. Not a philosophy of *mine* but of *ours*. Making room for the other person's reality is to engage in communication practices that respectfully acknowledge the individual worth of a person and the person's right to their own perspective while affirming your right to the way you are experiencing the situation. It is a consistent state of empathy, a *feeling into*. How do we empathize? We listen. Empathetic listening is listening with your mind and heart.

Key #4

Consistently Engage in Active, Empathetic Listening

All interpersonal relationships require the primary ingredient of active listening. Most experiences during the workday require that we listen. Active Listening is a skill vital to a cohesive, smooth-functioning organization. There is a vital connection between communication and listening. Listening is the other half, 50 percent of the effective communication experience. Of the four types of communication experiences you engage in daily, listening is practiced more than the other three (writing, speaking, and reading). According to sociocultural anthropologist Edward T. Hall, the United States operates as a *high-context society.* Such a society is very verbal and its members feel a consistent need to express their viewpoints. The cultural value of individualism further conditions us to always want to assert the "personal agenda." This makes it more difficult to make room for the other person's reality. Individualism is an important trait for success in a competitive society, but when exaggerated out of balance it becomes detrimental to creating caring, respectful relationships. Take a moment to examine your listening quotient by monitoring the bad listening habits in Application 3.4.

Listening: The Silent Healer

Listening requires four basic human elements: *mind, ears, eyes,* and *memory,* with all four working simultaneously to receive maximum input. Mind is the world of intellect and emotion housed in the brain. You need a brain to hear, but you need a mind to listen. The eyes reveal the true intent of an individual's behavior, motive, and feelings. The eyes cue us into what is revealed through nonverbal communication. We are always listening with our eyes. Where your eyes are, there your mind is! Your memory is the computer chip that drives the daily awareness of your surroundings. It is what you rely on most in the listening experience. Without memory, the other ingredients

Application 3.4 - Listening Self-Evaluation

Do you possess these problem habits and to what degree?
—Giving into internal noise
—Giving into external noise
—Judging a person by appearance
—Judging a person based on vocal sound: regional or ethnic dialect, accent, vocalics
—Faking paying attention
—Rejecting the speaker's message because of past experiences or personal prejudice
—Not paying attention to the speaker's evidence
—Jumping to conclusions
—Interrupting
—Not focusing on the speaker's major points

would have no reference. Ears that perform their physiological function are a blessing, but of all the ingredients listed, they do the least to aid the listening experience—not hearing, listening. Take care of your mind, body, and soul!

Understand that every time you listen, you *choose* to. Listening is a skill. It is an acquired ability. The deaf listen even though they cannot hear. As talking is to hearing, on a purely physiological level, so is communicating to listening, but on a purely intellectual level. Many know someone who has *talked* themselves out of a relationship or job, but few have ever *listened* themselves out of one!

Every situation does not require the same type or level of listening. We listen to information to understand or comprehend. We listen for appreciation to those things we like (e.g., music). We listen to empathize with those we share reality with. We listen to make critical decisions. These four listening arenas require all four of the aforementioned basic components but not all with the same intensity, because in each there is a different objective.

We utilize each of these listening experiences in our work environment daily. We spend hundreds of hours each year in meetings to comprehend the information provided to meet departmental goals. We catch up with our coworkers during the lunch break to talk over the latest family drama, seeking the empathy we crave. We have fiscal discussions so that we can listen and make the critical decisions regarding how to grow. We appreciate hearing that final whistle to go home! All day long, we are moving from one listening setting to another. On the way from one to the other, we need to consider the listening setting in order to be ready for the exchange. On the way to your next listening site, ask yourself, "How much do I need to engage in critical listening?" We do not need the same *presentness* when listening for enjoyment as we would if listening to information needed to make a decision. Listening to friends' woes requires a different level of cognition and absorption, through the heart. So, when we listen, we need to BE READY. Know where you are headed and what is expected of you in the listening experience. When you think about it, every communication experience is a listening experience. Are you treating it as such?

Be careful to adopt *listening behaviors* as opposed to *non-listening behaviors*. Sample lists of such behaviors are listed in Application 3.5.

It is also important to understand the role of the basic communication model in the effective listening experience. You can utilize the seven ingredients of the basic dyadic model to assess their effects or reflect about the listening experience. If you choose the wrong channel, encounter too much noise, or choose the wrong place, the listening process will be greatly disrupted. As encoders, we must create a communication environment receptive to listening. Manipulating the basic ingredients helps assure a positive outcome. It is a very old and true proverb, "Think before you speak." Unfortunately, not many

Application 3.5 - Listening Behaviors

Listening Behaviors	Nonlistening Behaviors
• Looking directly at the speaker	• Consistently looking away from the speaker
• Body is facing the speaker	• Allowing intrapersonal noise to take over (daydreaming)
• Using responsive Nonverbal Communication	
	• Interrupting
• Maintaining an open, pleasant facial expression	• Paying attention to mental and physical distractions and environment
• Reducing intrapersonal noise	• Fidgeting
	• Nonexpressive face and body
• Tracking main points	• Reading, watching TV, and other distractions
• Using your eyes, ears, mind, and memory	• Paying attention to the speaker's vocal or physical limitations instead of the message

know *what* to think about. What channel would you choose to discuss that sensitive issue with your office mate—a note on a desk? Decide if this is the right time to talk with your supervisor. What type of internal noise will try and invade the communication? Understanding and using these tools of listening effectiveness will ensure communication success in the workplace.

We need to keep our listening skills tuned up. Our families, our jobs, our social commitments rely on our ability to be truly *present*. We must learn to listen mentally and physically. Involve the senses in the listening experience. Be present. Our culture forces us to constantly dwell on the future; as a result, being in the present is a difficult task for most. But it is only in the NOW that we experience our relationships, our lives, to the fullest. Your professional success depends on how you think, speak, and act today, not what you think concerning tomorrow. Actually, there is no tomorrow: when you arrive there, it is again today. Effective listening involves being present with the one you are engaging with. You cannot make room for another person's reality if you do not listen. Nor can you be an effective communicator.

It is impossible to have professional success and be a poor listener.

A word concerning empathetic listening. Most of us have a basic understanding between the attributes of sympathy versus empathy. However, very few can easily transition between the feelings of pity for a situation to the feeling of connectedness and active concern required on the empathetic level. We are able to experience empathy most effectively in our personal relationships. Is there ever a time in the workplace where empathetic listening would better advance the relationship between coworkers? Take for example the coworker who has just experienced a family tragedy and returned to work unprepared to meet the impending project deadline. How do you react as a member of the team? Are you engaged in empathetic listening and thus ready to engage in active concern? Maybe the situation calls for you to step in and provide greater support to the project. Or maybe you may need to help the team reevaluate the deadline based on your coworker's readiness. The point here is that there are times when our interpersonal relationships at work require that we listen and respond with sincere feeling and concern. We all need a little extra support from time to time. When you are there for others, chances are others will be there for you.

Work relationships are interpersonal relationships, and interpersonal relationships are about communication, and communication is about listening. It is never too late to improve your listening skills. You will experience a more effective

83

communication environment and greater professional success when you become a better listener:

Ways to Become a Better Listener

- Refrain from interrupting
- Keep an open mind for other points of view
- Read
- Improve vocabulary
- Listen for main ideas
- Quiet internal noise
- Quiet external noise
- Be ready to listen
- Understand the level of listening required for each listening arena
- Withhold judgment and evaluation
- Use your eyes, ears, mind, memory
- Concentrate and pay attention
- Respect the sender
- Develop an interest in the topic
- Ask questions

Key #5

Live and Share the Platinum Rule

Key #5 has genuinely enhanced my ability to experience meaningful interpersonal relationships at home and at work, and it will do the same for you. It adds further to our ability to make room for the reality of another. The key concerns the *Platinum Rule* versus the *Golden Rule*. Most of us grew up being taught the Golden Rule: "Do unto others as you would have them to do unto you." This is a rule that affirms the worth of all living creatures. It is a good rule. It is a rule I try to apply broadly and generously in my life, as many do. However, the co-stars and other supporting cast members in our lives deserve better. Better? Yes, much better.

Practicing the Golden Rule, we do not necessarily have to *listen* to the needs, wants, or desires of the other person. Often it can lead to making the everyday assumptions we all have about what we *think* our partners want, need, or should have, too rarely acknowledging the fact that they are quite capable of letting us know what they want if we would just ask. I remember viewing John Gray's video, *Men Are from Mars, Women Are from Venus,* and there was this one couple having marriage problems that basically boiled down to their taking each other for granted. In one part of the discussion, the wife complained because the husband never gave her flowers, not even when she gave birth to their children. She was highly offended and grieved by what she felt was his lack of compassion and caring. The husband on the other hand did not see what the big deal was about flowers. He gave her other gifts through the years, much more expensive ones, and as long as she harped on him about giving her flowers, he was not going to. He was not exercising empathetic listening, but saw himself as exercising the Golden Rule. He got her what he wanted her to have. Hmmm . . .

Well, the Platinum Rule (as discussed by Milton Bennett in *Looking Out, Looking In*) in effect elevates the Golden Rule while not diminishing its importance. It states, "Do unto others as *they* would have you to do unto them." This rule requires that we stop, then look and listen with our hearts for the needs of others. It is the byproduct of making room for another person's reality. It definitely would do a lot for work relations, not to mention our homes and our communities. Have you ever known a colleague whom everyone in the organization valued because of their ability to anticipate the needs of those around them? How about the individual who shows up to the meeting with extra copies or pastry for everyone? Imagine leadership so in tune with their team that they are already looking for opportunities to help their team grow and advance. Think about it.

Application 3.6 - The Platinum Rule

Choose a coworker you feel comfortable with and practice the Platinum Rule for one week.

Observe with your eyes and heart how you support your coworker. Look for opportunities to anticipate the things that you can do to help give them relief or comfort.

One week is all you need to see fantastic changes in your attitude and theirs!

Apply the Platinum Rule in Application 3.6 in your interpersonal work relationships and watch their quality change almost overnight. Lead by example and others will follow.

The third step in the Communication Staircase vibrates throughout every aspect of our human relationship experience. We express the positive communication principles of Interpersonal Communication through these five (5) important keys:

Five Keys to Positive, Healthy Interpersonal Relationships

- Be the person you want to work with!
- Choose the right people, make the right connections.
- Make room for the *other person's reality.*
- Maintain active, *empathetic listening.*
- Allow the *Platinum Rule* to be your rule of thumb.

As a result of your intrapersonal health, your nonverbal awareness, and your interpersonal skills, you can move more comfortably and confidently onto the next steps of daily communication. These next steps move into the realm of interaction within groups according to the daily script of your life. Here you can put to work the effective communication skills you are using to reshape your life and broaden your professional horizons. Apply the concepts discussed in this chapter and experience a richer, fuller movie with a cast of your choice!

Q & A Interpersonal Communication

Dear PS,

Q: I would like to know how to tactfully tell a coworker his conflict-management skills are really poor. He really hates any perceived criticism and flies off the handle quickly.

A: Your language is a bit strong and I am not sure if you should talk to this individual without an intervening, concurring partner. If this is someone you feel comfortable and have a rapport with, then yes, find a good time (situation/context) to voice your concern to your coworker IF you really feel that this is something that can help his employment situation. Start with something like, "John, you are a really passionate guy and it's one of the reasons I admire your work. . . ." You may suggest that you were thinking about taking a company Co-opetition Communication Course (CCC™) and would like him to join you. (See my discussion of co-opetition in Chapter 4.)

Q: I have a real hard time talking with coworkers one on one. When we are in meetings or small groups I am OK, but when I have to interact interpersonally, I don't know what to say!

A: The art of conversation is a skill that escapes most people for a number of reasons. One wonderful interpersonal conversation resource is listening! You'd be surprised what you can relate to when you recognize the commonness found in most discussions. Another important guide to conversation is your repertoire. What are your interests? What do you know? What can you converse about? Discover a little about a lot and feel more comfortable talking to anyone! Lastly, learn to value silence. You do not have to say anything unless you feel it worthwhile for all listening.

Q: My friend at work has a terrible habit of interrupting people while they are talking. She often uses the excuse she will forget her point if she doesn't share it immediately. Is this a valid excuse? I have heard many people use it.

A: Whenever someone interrupts another person, no matter the circumstances, they are in effect saying, "My thoughts and concerns are more valid or important than yours." Yes, emergency cases present themselves where interruption is valid, but this is not usually the case in the business paradigm. We understand that it is mostly the noise in an individual's head that refuses to be silenced when listening to others. Have her read the section in this chapter on listening and take the Listening Self-assessment Examination. Hopefully, she will be able to see herself with honest assessment. And of course, "excuse me" always helps!

Q: I think I made a bad decision to be aligned with a coworker who has a reputation for being hard to work with. She often has legitimate points of what's wrong with things, but chooses to share her concerns in a manner that puts others off. I am worried that my connection to her might damage my professional image.

A: You have cause for concern if you are seen as a supporter of your colleague's negative image. It is obviously time to have a serious conversation about the need to learn tact, diplomacy, and restraint in how she brings her concerns to the forefront. If she is hostile and unchanging during this discussion, respectfully let her know that your decision to dealign yourself with her is not personal but is done only in your professional best interest.

Q: My supervisor's conflict-management style is terrible. He often berates workers in front of others and is quick to find fault even for the smallest of infractions. My division is really suffering from low morale.

A: Many employees find themselves being subjected to individuals who have been given the power to lead without the skill. If this is a collective concern, ask to have a division meeting to air concerns in a manner that does not place blame or focus on the offender but instead opens the floor to discussion of how the communication climate in the division can be improved. People find it difficult to be the brunt of criticism but will often listen and internalize what they perceive to be a common issue everyone is trying to address.

Small-Group/ Organizational Communication

"A threefold cord is not easily broken."
—Ecclesiastes 4:12

TO GROUP OR NOT TO GROUP . . . THAT IS THE QUESTION

I recently engaged in a conversation with a college student who shared her absolute disdain for group projects because there are always "the strong students and the weak students, and the harder-working students have to shoulder the burden of the weaker ones. It's not fair!" This was a reoccurring chorus from many individuals required to take the Small-Group Communication class. I told the student, "Yes, there will be stronger and weaker contributors in a group, but I do not agree that it's not fair to require this type of group work." She looked at me

91

with this look of "what planet did you come from?" I continued, "When you are working for a company that has a variety of departments dependent on one another to create a complete product, you are only as valuable as your contribution to the whole. Can you make the company successful alone?" Interestingly enough, though Small-Group Communication was always the smallest of my classes, it was also one of the most impacting. Individuals shed tears when it was time to part. They had come to understand the value and joy of working with others. Exactly how do we get things done in a society where individuals are hyperindividualistic, highly competitive, and fearful of working with others?

This is not an uncommon discussion when dealing with the subject of teamwork. Out of the Los Angeles riots of 1992 came a now commonly used phrase: "Why can't we all just get along?" Why can't we? Small-Group, or Organizational Communication, can be defined as communication *that includes multiple perspectives, all trying to achieve goals that can be seen as both personally and collectively beneficial.* This fourth step of effective communication requires that we write into our daily script the personal integrity, confidence, and communication skills necessary to be effective in our group settings. Organizational members often wonder what makes a winning team or organization. The answer is simple but the hardest formula for many organizations to achieve:

 A winning team is composed of members who contribute their individual best collectively!

JILL'S DAY

Remember Jill's group experience? Can you see how Jill's failure to bring her individual best to the afternoon meeting precluded her chances of a successful experience? What if Jill had not woken up on the wrong side of the bed and continued her morning in a disgruntled manner? What if she had been able to wear the outfit she planned and felt good about her appearance? How do you think these communication experiences may have impacted her mood at the afternoon department meeting? The noise in her head prevented her from being open to other perspectives in the group. She engaged in selective listening from the onset. Jill brought this attitude with her to the experience and looked for validation of her dissatisfaction throughout. Replay for yourself how your day progresses into an experience self-created. Do you have an *afternoon mood?* Replace it with your purposeful thoughts of team productivity and self-satisfaction.

I VERSUS *WE:* THE CULTURAL PARADOX

As we strive to individually contribute to the collective best, we must understand why it is difficult for many to do so. What are the patterns and habits that have become the hallmarks of self-preservation? Many of us have been enculturated into the value system of *individualism.* An individualistic culture sees *the individual as the single most important unit of the society.* From individualism we create free enterprise, competition, democracy, equality, materialism, and many other expressions of the liberties of the single unit. Individual rights and freedoms are paramount to the ideal of a democratic society. To this end, we set up our organizations to in some way become an economic expression of the values that are important to our worldview. These ideals become the way we do business with others. The other end of the spectrum reveals cultures that are *collective* in nature and establish the society based on *in-groups* versus *out-groups.* The family, clan, or tribe is the most important unit to the society. Individual rights are secondary to the good or survival of the in-group. Members of the in-group work together

93

cooperatively. The out-group is that clan, tribe, or group that does not share the in-group's point of reference or worldview.

There are benefits to both individualism and collectivism, depending on how a society makes use of them. However, these ideologies can also lead to complex social and political concerns. For instance, under the guise of individual freedom the push toward conformity still prevails. Two examples would be the narrowly defined concepts of success and beauty. The "every man for himself" competitive philosophy many adopt in the workplace to get ahead is not one that encourages the team or group ethic. This can be and is often very damaging to the vital unity of the organization. There is also the narrow dominant perspective of beauty, which creates a very sterile culture regarding what is defined as appealing or acceptable. This is very prevalent in the workplace, as witnessed in Chapter 2 under the discussion on appearance. Imagine how many individuals from varying cultures adjust their ethnic look or attire to fit into the "corporate look." So whereas we say we value individualism and prize equality, we do so only within the constraints created by those in charge. There are many individuals who feel they do not *personally* contribute to the organizational culture. They believe they are required to merely fit in. How can they bring their individual best and blossom to contribute to the collective success? (See Application 4.1.)

Within the cultural framework of collective societies, many are strongly encouraged to conform to the will of the group. And, yes, sometimes in a way that negates individual voices. There can be the danger of groupthink. Collective societies encourage members to subject their individual desires to the collective need. Various forms of autocratic leadership are often prevalent in collective cultures. These cultures are more homogeneous and strongly encourage members to conform for the good of the group, to maintain traditions and ancestral values. It is the in-group that matters. Here we do have the sacrifice of self for the group; however, one must still be a part of THE in-

Application 4.1 - Individualism and You

How important is individualism to you? Have you ever thought about the impact this concept has on the organization?

What ways do you advance the focus of individualism in your department? Are you a team player? Do you make sure others take note of YOUR efforts even when the project clearly was a team effort?

Taking an inventory of how much you value individualism and allow it to play a role in your group dynamics will definitely help you to see the need to balance this trait against the needs of the group and organization.

group. Ethnocentrism exists everywhere. Read Chapter 7 to engage in this discussion further.

CO-OPETITION MODEL OF ADVANCEMENT

When examining our work environments, we foster organizations that encourage individual competition but rely on group efforts and cooperation. Statistics on company failures, employee attrition, and turnover rates provide evidence that there is imbalance in the areas of competition versus cooperation. Is it one or the other? We see there is still the proclivity, no matter which ideology, to not hear the other perspective if it is not rooted in your own worldview. Both sides unchecked can lead to extremism. Is there a middle ground? The combination of cooperation and competition creates a synergistic model of *co-opetition,* a term coined by Raymond John "Ray" Noorda, the CEO of Novell between 1982 and 1994.

Within the Small-Group Communication setting, I define co-opetition as the need for every person to contribute their individual best to the collective. We can recognize co-opetition in the workplace because members of the organizational culture begin to own the experience they are having. They begin to recognize their self-contribution and the equally valuable contributions of others. This translates into communication patterns that are both self-affirming and climate supportive. We will begin to foster institutions that create collective merit systems that recognize the contributions of the whole group on a project. Too often we single out individuals, when behind them stood a number of others who helped to carry the torch. I have often envisioned participating in a game show where the winner would be the team that did the most to help the opposing side, AND both sides would win prizes. The questions or exercises would be challenging and stimulate a lot of excitement, but co-opetition would be the driving force (see Application 4.2). Some may say, "Ahhh, here we go again! Competition is good for you! You need to be assertive!" Maybe, but remember: too much of anything ain't a good thing.

Application 4.2 - Co-opetition Project

Have a contest! Come up with a good work project that you need completed; maybe a quarterly review of the communication flow within the organization.

Get all the departments to work together to prepare the report for management. Give "co-opetition points" to the division that supports the others' efforts.

Allow the project to transpire over a period of time so there is no heightened stress. Reward a bonus for team effectiveness and synergy for the final report and the group that receives the most co-opetition points.

MAKING ROOM FOR THE GROUP REALITY

Small-Group Communication requires a broadening of our communication abilities to include three or more perspectives, all operating from different perspectives, which are often assumed to be compatible. When engaging in group communication, just as with interpersonal communication, we bring with us the intrapersonal health of our individual selves as well as the interpersonal skills we have adopted with those in our life movie. Think about how the seven basic ingredients of the communication experience are enhanced when more than two individuals are contributing to the noise, decoding according to their particular viewpoints, and giving back different nonverbal feedback. The need to make room for the other person's reality is magnified within the small-group dynamic because most individuals have perceived and already solved the problem based on their personal reality and personal needs. For better or for worse, the hyper-individualistic culture we live in propagates a whole culture of people very adept at surface communication, conflict avoidance, and adopting passive-aggressive types of defense mechanisms. We experience little "blowups" in our communication environments every day due to the inability to make room for multiple points of view, and due to ineffective communication skills. We are taught to compete with one another more often than we are taught to work together for the greater good.

Daily we witness the stress many feel to make the grade. The desire to achieve a pat on the back often propagates self-centered ambitions. This is often compounded by the atmosphere of competition most workers thrive in. However, in spite of all this individualistic competition, we manage to maintain the institutions we thrive in with a modicum of success others wish to emulate. We are able to do this through the vision and abilities of those who lead their teams to a unified objective, realizing there is no "I" in team. We are able to do this because we are a nation of individuals who singularly desire to achieve their professional dreams and goals. Increasingly, the dynamics of the

97

global village and global economy create interesting challenges for doing business worldwide. Why are some individuals extremely successful within the corporate or institutional dynamic while others appear to be stagnant, with no apparent vested interest? These leaders have a fundamental understanding that drives their decision-making skills. It is the understanding that effective communication practices are the keys to a successful organization. Show me an organization that does not have a structured, organized communication chart/flow and I will show you an organization that has failed or is failing.

So here you are within the department, the organization, trying to fit in, trying to be heard. The same personal issues that go into dyadic communication often surface in the group dynamic: insecurities, intrapersonal noise, prejudices, failure to perceive value in other perspectives, and so on. The more points of view that have to be considered in the discussion, the greater the need for problem-solving and conflict-management skills. Our families and communities do not offer enough positive examples of conflict resolution, and too much of what we experience is based on aggressive, win-lose patterns of resolution. A type of only-one-can-be-the-victor attitude. Most dredge up from the bottom of their lakes the same type of conflict-resolution skills they used as children or the same coping skills they mimicked from adults in their young lives. How can we have harmony within our institutions if we do not have harmony within ourselves, within our homes? We must all learn that "getting along" is a matter of setting aside personal points of view long enough to make room for the fact that there is always more than one way to approach any discussion, any solution. As within the interpersonal dynamic, critical listening and thinking skills are paramount to group communication.

LEADERSHIP COMMUNICATION

Regardless of systems put in place designed to advance organizational goals, success lies solidly on the backs of those in leadership positions charged with the mandate to get the job done. How do leaders get the job done? Communication lies at the foundation of all effective leadership. This is the major reason this book brings communication-as-system to the forefront in examining organizational productivity. The aim is to understand the complexities of communication in all of its arenas and offer a more unifying approach as to how communication functions on all levels—internally and externally. The organizational leader must know and work to advance the institution within this framework.

In order to facilitate an effective communication climate, those responsible must take the steps to achieve their own level of comfort and skill. We are all familiar with the saying the "blind leading the blind." Too often those who lead organizations have not done the necessary homework to make sure their communication abilities and usage are not damaging to those they are trying to lead. What type of leader are you required to be? Organizations and groups need varying leadership styles. Maybe yours is a social group and needs only laissez-faire leadership—leadership that acts only to serve as an anchor, not necessarily a guide, a nonbinding glue that provides a common base. Or maybe you must exercise *authoritarian* leadership and consciously, vigorously direct your organization. You are the helm of the ship. Everyone takes their direction from your vision. Do you have one? Then there are groups that function more productively in *democratic* leadership environments. These organizations feel it necessary to allow most members to know they have a recognized individual contribution. Democratic leadership requires methods in place for including everyone at all levels of the organization in the creative and decision-making process. Unfortunately, there also times when *abdacratic* leadership exists, and that is basically no leadership at all. We witness many organizations fail from this problem. Regardless of the type of leadership mandated by your organization or group, you need to be prepared for the communication responsibility and expertise required to be an effective leader.

Leadership is who you are and not what you are.

How major a role does communication play concerning your leadership style? What is your leadership voice? Is it confident? Strong? Willing to admit mistakes and consider differing points of view? What about your tone? Review Chapter 2 and the section on paralanguage—understanding the impact of not *what* but *how* you say what you say. Volume, tone, pacing, dialect, and many other vocal characteristics play a role in how people perceive you, based on their conditioning. What type of language do you use? Your communication should be purposeful and affirming to yourself and those you are leading! Sincerely and with integrity, support those you can. Help to guide the others onward. Allow your "yes" to be yes and your "no" to be no. Your actions should be a direct reflection of your word. Your word should directly mirror your actions (see Application 4.3).

Become aware of your communication style and request feedback to assess this vital area of leadership. Adopt Leadership Communication practices that positively impact the company's health. Using *intent-driven* and *esteem-building* language is needed to replace communication that is toxic and ego damaging. Examples of intent-driven and supportive communication include:

Intent Driven	Esteem Building
The organization WILL meet its goal of . . .	Communicating as equals
Employer and employees are working together . . .	Proactive conflict resolution
We are a team of multiple perspectives with common goals . . .	Consistent praise

Application 4.3 - Leadership Communication

Self-Monitoring Questions:

- How would you judge your ability to communicate with those you have a responsibility to lead?
- More importantly, how would they judge your ability to lead?
- What type of leadership communication do you use?
- Is there integrity associated with my word?
- Are you affirming?
- Do you have a strong sense of confidence about yourself and the company you are working for, so much that it shows to all who work with you?
- Is there passion in your words and actions?
- How is your self-talk?
- With what intent do you face your employees each day?
- How is your crisis communication?

Intent Driven	Esteem Building
Our work together has furthered . . .	Direct, clear feedback
We will accomplish . . .	Descriptive, *I/we* versus *you*

Accepting the privileges and challenges of being a good leader requires that we use our communication expertise to always encourage productive, passion-filled organizational environments. Your thoughts, words, and actions create and support the leadership identity you determine.

CONSTRUCTIVE CONFLICT

Conflict is a reasonable expectation under any group dynamic. As discussed in Chapter 3, conflict is normal when two or more

101

viewpoints have a vested interest in the outcome of a decision. One primary consideration of workplace conflict is that all members should have as their major concern the good of the organization. Ultimately, the decision that best advances the goal of the institution should prevail. A knowledgeable group leader skilled in conflict management and mediation will be able to move the group forward to the collective goal. There are a variety of group-conflict methods available for facilitators. Despite the different methodologies, most resolution patterns have as their basis the same precise steps:

Group Problem Solving Method

- Defining the problem so that everyone is on the same page
- Understanding the issues that comprise the problem
- Reviewing group and organizational resources to solve the problem
- Setting an agenda to gather information and resources to solve the problem
- Applying a solution to remedy the problem

As long as members maintain a "team" attitude and bring their individual best for the collective good, the group should be able to come to a solution that is a consensus.

THE COMMUNICATION CLIMATE

Within the organizational dynamic, we have *formal* and *informal communication networks*. These networks allow both structured and unstructured flow of communication, from management to labor, labor to management, coworker to coworker, and company to client. Formal structures include the company's policies, rules, tracking systems, evaluation processes, complaint processes, and all other aspects of communication as formally mandated through company policy. There is often a handbook that new employees receive to explain the formal communication process.

The informal structures are those that exist without benefit of policy, but they have just as much to do with the communication dynamics of the organization as the formal structures. Informal communication practices include discussions in the break room or cafeteria, at the water cooler or company picnic, the *gossip* that clarifies what really went on behind the closed doors, the chat with a colleague who can help you expedite some red tape. Any wise manager realizes that informal communication is just as important to the organizational dynamic as formal communication. A lot of what goes on is "heard through the grapevine." Often the informal communication acts as the "central nervous system" of the organization. A formal/informal communication flow chart may look something like the diagram in Figure 4.1.

There is a constant interplay between the areas of formal and informal networks. As a result, the communication environment must be managed in a way that takes into account both of these vital areas within the organization. Often, when conducting Communication Audits within an organization, we are surprised to find how much the information flowing from informal networks can positively or adversely affect the organizational context. From office chatter to lunchroom grapevines, communication travels through the network of the organization, impacting relationships, morale, and productivity. Become skilled at using both the formal and informal channels to learn from and influence the communication climate.

Depending on the formal or informal flow of communication, there are patterns of communication that will support your group communications in a more conducive manner than another pattern might. These patterns of information dissemination determine how individuals receive and use the information shared. Examine Figure 4.2 and notice the patterns that support

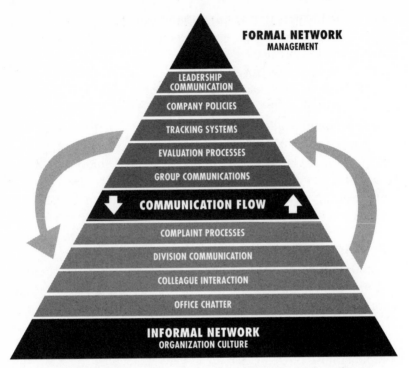

Figure 4.1 Organizational Communications Flow Chart

a more formal climate versus a climate that is more social. The patterns are arranged from the most formal to the least formal, the most rigid structure to the least rigid structure.

Top down is the typical organizational hierarchical pattern: board of directors, president, VPs, managers, and on down, all vertical. This facilitates formal communication patterns. The *forward pattern* moves communication along a designed, formal line of information sharing. It carries the organization forward horizontally. Then the *circle pattern* broadens the outreach by widening the table of those allowed to participate; it tends more toward the informal, but is somewhat closed. The *social pattern* is an open, active network of exchange generally utilized for informal, social group discussions. It is important that the organization be aware of the various patterns of group

TYPICAL ORGANIZATIONAL PATTERNS

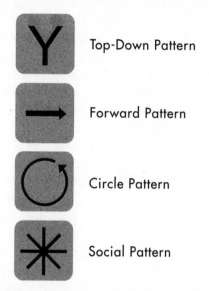

Top-Down Pattern

Forward Pattern

Circle Pattern

Social Pattern

Figure 4.2 Organizational Communication Patterns

communication and how these can function to advance the aim of effective communication. Choosing the appropriate communication pattern for a specific group experience can help facilitate positive group communication efforts.

Now let's return to the seven basic ingredients of dyadic communication and add the multiple perspectives you might experience in a meeting or a social gathering. These seven ingredients of sender, message, channel, situation, noise, listener, and feedback are very much a part of the group communication climate. Think about how the situation or setting affects the mood of communication. What about the time of day? How do you react to training first thing in the morning versus after lunch versus at the end of the day? These factors will greatly impact how you and others receive the message being communicated. Have you considered noise that could be cross-cultural in origin such as individualistic versus collective perspectives? Or group spatial relationships based on cultural socialization might determine who is comfortable next to whom. Are you adept at reading group feedback? It is important for the team leader to discern what type of internal noise may present itself at the meeting through the individual attendees. Being able to manipulate these simple but vital ingredients can make a huge difference in group communication effectiveness. Understanding the seven basic ingredients will increase your ease in communicating within a group effectively.

SMALL-GROUP MEMBERSHIP AND FACILITATION

There are numerous problem-solving and conflict-resolution methods supporting successful group interaction and decision making. Successful group interaction is a complex mix of seven (7) elements: (1) healthy personal outlooks, (2) effective communication skills, (3) shared commitment to goals, (4) teamwork ethics, (5) group-communication ability, (6) maintenance tasks, and (7) conflict-management skills. A team must include members who are adept at group-communication practices. Effective facilitation is a skill. Make sure you have a good guidebook for templates of professional agendas, meeting checklists, technical and group needs, and minutes. The skilled use of parliamentary procedure is necessary to move forward respectful group interaction, decision making, and problem solving. Group methods such as brainstorming, roundtable discussions, buzz sessions, reflective critical thinking, committees, and other approaches do work when managed by knowledgeable facilitators.

Constructively examine your ability to work as part of a group whether its setting is personal, social, or professional. How are you doing? Can you see the connection between your personal self-worth and how you relate to others? We know that the mirror messages we receive within the group experience reflect the personal messages we send out. Have you written a script for your daily and long-term goals with the firm?

When conflicts arise, do you immediately get defensive, passive, antagonistic? Have you learned to deal with conflict constructively and maturely? These are skills most of us just do not have! Couple that lack with the high value we place on individualism, and it sometimes appears work life is a constant struggle of wills. However, the experience starts and ends with you. Remember, you bring *you* to the table. Make sure you are the team player you would want to work with. You can help create a communication environment that you and others can flourish in. It's just another scene in your life movie.

Productive and progressive membership is essential. Being a great team member requires your dedication to five (5) elements: (1) the goals of the group, (2) the ethical leadership of the group, (3) the team's membership, (4) the team's daily productivity, and (5) the harmony of the group. All groups go through the same basic steps when finding their synergy: coming together; resistance; conforming; and, lastly, stabilizing into their particular group dynamic. It takes time and commitment to effectively add to a team, but everyone can make a positive contribution. Make sure you know what you bring to the group dynamic. You have power to advance the group's mission. Maybe you have *Influence Power, Information Power, Technical Power, Marketing Power, Logistics Power, Relationship Power, Stay-the-Course Power,* etc. Find your power and add it to the mix! You do this by tapping into the thoughts, words, and actions that exemplify who you are. Find your voice! Your expert communication is the major contribution to the team's successful mission.

You have successfully maneuvered the first four steps of the Communication Staircase Model. After working to create the positive and productive self, you are now ready to face your public!

Bring your individual best to the collective good!

Q & A Small-Group/Organizational Communication

Dear PS,

Q: Employee morale is at an all-time low. We have suffered major organizational restructuring to prevent company closure. Many invested workers were given early release, and those who survived are sullen, fearful, even hostile. Any advice?

A: You of course realize that your organization is one of thousands experiencing the same concerns in this fragile global economy. Despite the need to push forward and demand everyone stay focused on the tasks at hand, your institution must take the time to assess and regain a supportive communication climate. Set up informal luncheon forums that allow everyone to be heard in an atmosphere of collective support. Keepers of the "suggestion box" should encourage and attend to voiced concerns. The major issue is to make sure all members see and experience a concerted effort on the part of management to acknowledge and be a part of the healing process in a way that works best for your organization.

Q: I am a small-group facilitator working with a group that is very diverse. I don't just mean ethnically, but all types of attitudes and cultural variations. To top it off, there are two coworkers in the group who have experienced unpleasant interaction in the past.

A: Group facilitation can be very challenging and should be undertaken by trained individuals. Make sure that you take advantage of professional-development opportunities in facilitation skills. The major thrust of any good group leadership is your belief and passion about the project. This will become infectious to the other members and encourage them to bring their individual best. Be careful to work on the maintenance needs of the group: interpersonal relationships, conflict management, praise, and intent communication. These habits will go a long way to defuse any hyper-individualistic tendencies. Make sure that concerns are immediately and openly addressed by the entire group. Use your expertise to keep members focused on tasks and not personalities.

Q: We have a member of our team who is downright lazy. I am tired of pulling this guy's weight. I tried to talk to the manager, but she keeps saying to give it some time.

A: Your group leader should take time to bring forward the unproductive member's team contribution. What is his talent, his passion? Can the team benefit from it? Team members should encourage support and input. Have you ever considered that there are those who need more support than others for a variety of reasons? Are we our brothers' keepers? A society prospers as it takes care of its widows, orphans, voiceless, and weak. Sometimes we will be required to go the extra mile.

Q: I never know what to say in a group. I always feel out of place. I try to be social, but I just don't feel comfortable.

A: Review the information shared in Chapter 1 on building your self-esteem and in Chapter 5 on the art of conversation. It is important to find your voice in any situation where you feel you want to contribute. The gift of gab does not belong to the few but is a learned art available to everyone. Build your self-confidence and your conversational repertoire.

Q: My team never seems to be able to solve conflicts. We always get what I call "personality jammed."

A: This goes back to the basic premise of this chapter: finding a balance between the hyperindividualism that drives many in our culture and the need to become more collective in our group goals. Share the information in this chapter with the group leader and other members. Engage others in a discussion on the organizational values and mores that might be damaging to the group process, and the need to recognize the organization's ability to make adjustments to advance the goals of the group.

Public Communication

We wear the mask that grins and lies; it hides our cheeks and shades our eyes . . . .

—Paul Laurence Dunbar

THE COMMON DENOMINATOR

The above excerpt from the poem "We Wear the Mask" aptly describes the manner in which most of us meet and greet the world on a daily basis. As we leave the safety of our personal spaces, we gear up to face a world where we must meet a variety of responsibilities and wear a variety of hats. As a result, most people *wear the masks* that help them rise to the occasion and meet the manifold pressures they are required to perform. Public speaking has been touted as the *number-one* fear known to man. Yes, people are more afraid of speaking publicly than falling into a pit of live snakes, bungee jumping,

111

or—in some cases—even dying! You've heard people say, "I'd rather die!" Fear of speaking in public is a common phenomenon in many cultures. How comfortable do you feel expressing yourself in front of a group? How would you rate your public communication effectiveness on a scale of one through eight, with eight being exceptional?

Public Communication is the *act of communicating publicly in a private or open forum, whether to inform, persuade, or entertain.* There are a variety of communication circumstances that require we speak publicly whether we want to or not. Interviewing, department meetings, business gatherings, and performance appraisals are all circumstances most of us will find ourselves in at some point during our adult lives. It is with this fifth step of effective communication that we find the power to pull together all of our communication resources and use our voices to perform and effect change! The business setting offers a variety of communication channels to address the business public. New technologies make it possible to engage in public speaking not just in front of a live audience but through a variety of mediums. Each channel has its unique requirement when it comes to expert delivery. There are definite do's and don'ts concerning the use of microphones, video, audio, and other voice- and image-capturing technology. It is important to know how to professionally use various *communication channels* so that you have some knowledge of how your clients are capable of getting your message AND how you come across in these mediums (see Figure 5.1). We all know about the YouTube craze. How are you at blogging, video streaming, phone conferencing, teleconferencing, texting, and other recently mass generated forms of communicating with the public?

MOVING BEYOND THE FEAR!

Public speaking is a learned and skilled ART! Too many individuals consign themselves to the back of the boardroom,

112

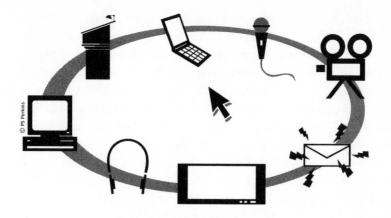

What is your medium of choice?

Figure 5.1 Communication Channels

meeting hall, classroom, or conference room in order to avoid being *called upon* or having to participate in the discussion. The majority of individuals would like to remain invisible and just absorb what is going on. Oh yes, they have plenty to say, and some will even sit and *stew* in their seats rather than offer a comment of insight or dissent. What makes the average person so afraid to engage in public discussion? Why do most experience a debilitating level of stage fright? It goes back to step one. Self-esteem and self-worth play major roles in our ability to function comfortably in front of others.

I remember a student almost ready to graduate with her four-year degree. She wanted to meet with me before the semester started. She had a concern she wanted to share. I will never forget the look of apprehension on her face and the nervousness in her voice as she shared with me what was one of the most difficult issues in her college career thus far. She stated, "I am due to graduate this spring with my degree in business management, and this class is the last class I need to graduate." I was a little perplexed as to why a senior waited so long to take a beginning-level communications class. I was even more appalled at the fact that her school did not require

113

more than a beginning-level communications class to prepare its graduates for the world of work! So here she was, trying to graduate after four years of never being required to develop her presentational skills. She went on to tell me the depth of the problem by relaying that she had attempted to take the class seven times! Each time she was called upon to give her first speech, she would get up and walk out of the class never to return. She was now obviously down to the wire, with no other alternative but to take the class and pass it with at least a C or better. Help!

Well, I love a challenge and can happily relate that through personal coaching and a classroom environment designed to minimize the "fear factor," she not only passed the class but enjoyed it, graduating with a B. Her final words to me were "Thanks so much for getting me through this. I do not know what I was so scared of!" I run into hundreds of professionals each year who would give their eyetooth not to have to speak publicly. And, for most, this fear of public address is definitely a detriment to their professional and public lives. How many opportunities do you miss on a daily basis because you are afraid to speak up? How many times have you been overlooked because you have not found your voice?

COMMUNICATION APPREHENSION

Fears and insecurities often surface when you are faced with judgment, evaluation, and possible criticism. We are constantly comparing ourselves among ourselves (social comparisons), and as a result we maintain a constant consciousness of being under a microscope. The scrutiny may not always be there, but nevertheless we have been conditioned to feel it's there. So many speakers share how uncomfortable they feel when people are *staring* at them. All of the deep, buried issues of criticism and inadequacy create an intolerable barrier for some to break through. We constantly replay the negative experiences

Application 5.1 - Practice! Practice! Practice!

Take every opportunity to volunteer to present on behalf of your department or group. Enlist the aid of others to prepare your message, but make sure you are comfortable and qualified to deliver the message.

Practice makes perfect!

of criticism we hold on to, those mirror messages that tell us we are not good enough. But remember, that voice you are listening to—it's yours! For some, that one bad experience becomes an overgeneralization that becomes the excuse to never speak publicly again. We often make the assumption that everyone is judging us, expecting us to make a mistake or fail. And what if we do make a mistake? So many are conditioned that the only allowed, possible outcome is success; failure is not an option. This, of course, is not realistic, just the flawed belief resulting from always needing to be perfect. Failure is often the door to success, if you stay the course. You cannot succeed unless you try, and sometimes it takes more than once to get it right. There are other falsely based assumptions that keep many from allowing their voices to be heard. It really boils down to confidence in one's self and the communication skill to express that confidence (see Application 5.1). Many have heard the acronym for FEAR—False Evidence Appearing Real! Most of your fears are based upon an unreal imagination of what-ifs. And even if the what-if surfaces, it is never as bad as the illusion your imagination wants to create.

CONFIDENCE *AND* COMPOSURE

Effective communicators are not born; they are trained. Few individuals have a natural talent for good communication. They may have the gift of gab, but that's not the same as effective communication. They must develop the personal and professional techniques that ensure public-presentation success. The first step is to understand the inside-out process of building personal confidence. Do you know the difference between confidence and composure? Most people consider them to be the same or cannot distinguish the difference.

Confidence is developed during the process of preparation. You are confident because you are ready. Composure is what you maintain DURING the presentation.

Some hire motivational coaches, others listen to self-help tapes, some attend specialized clinics, still others seek a qualified practitioner. Feeling confident and getting your message across in front of an audience are indeed valuable learned skills.

The following list of excellent presenters' characteristics introduces the skills you want to gain:

- Excellent presenters are message-conscious rather than self-conscious.
- Excellent presenters acquire active listening skills and understand that effective communicators are skilled listeners.
- Excellent presenters understand the principles of scholarly research and organization of ideas.
- Excellent presenters have a knowledgeable vocabulary that is consistently supplemented with the aid of a dictionary and thesaurus.
- Excellent presenters are aware of paralanguage and other nonverbal codes that make or break communication effectiveness.
- Excellent presenters focus on the clarity of words and understand that communication in all settings is either

appropriate or inappropriate, which allows for diverse communication arenas.

- Excellent presenters have a good repertoire of subjects they are familiar with, one that allows them to feel comfortable in most discussions they choose to engage in.
- Excellent presenters are comfortable with multicultural audiences due to the presenters' global awareness and respect for diversity.
- Excellent presenters enjoy the process of human communication. They understand the artistry of words.

Nervousness when speaking in public is normal. There is only one sure way to control nervousness or stage fright when speaking in public, and that is preparation—plain and simple. Being adequately prepared will help you maintain message-consciousness and focus on the point of your presentation. Preparation provides the confidence to face your audience and helps you maintain composure.

The shyness that can feel so overwhelming is just another way those negative voices try and discourage you from finding your voice. Do not focus on them. See all that and allow it to move on. Channel your thoughts elsewhere—on your message. You may experience physiological discomfort, such as dry mouth, sweaty palms, and rapid heart rate. These are just the signs that your body is ready to go into action. It is ready to perform! OK, so keep a glass of water close by, have a handkerchief and take deep breaths, and remember that all these body reactions are normal. Use these adrenaline cues to propel your energetic and enthusiastic presentation. Think of an Olympic athlete running for the gold medal. She needs the adrenaline to drive her body toward the finish line; without it she will not finish first. All professional presenters experience these discomforts, but they do not allow the feelings to debilitate them. They use the energy to their advantage. It is when they do not feel a level of anxious anticipation that they should be concerned (see Application 5.2).

Application 5.2 - Self-Confidence Quotient

Take this self-confidence measurement quiz:

1. I volunteer to speak at meetings.

   Never   Sometimes   Always
   0   1   2

2. I engage in impromptu discussions at work.

   Never   Sometimes   Always
   0   1   2

3. I am comfortable with my interpersonal skills.

   Never   Sometimes   Always
   0   1   2

4. I am confident speaking in front of groups.

   Never   Sometimes   Always
   0   1   2

5. I maintain composure even when nervous.

   Never   Sometimes   Always
   0   1   2

6. My public visual, vocal, and mental messages are congruent.

   Never   Sometimes   Always
   0   1   2

7. My job recognizes my ability to speak with confidence and expertise.

   Never   Sometimes   Always
   0   1   2

Score:

0–6:   Need coaching and confidence building support

7–10:   Good start; increase public speaking opportunities

11–14:   Great, seek more visibility to represent the company

Psychological preparation is a valuable tool to help you conquer communication apprehension. Envision yourself having the public speaking experience you desire. See yourself at the board meeting responding calmly to difficult questions. See yourself standing tall and delivering your message with passion and confidence! See the audience responding verbally and nonverbally with enthusiasm. Take every opportunity to speak in front of groups to improve your skills and become more confident. Take control of the FEAR by preparing yourself to face it! As coined by author Marianne Williamson and shared by famed activist President Nelson Mandela:

> Our worst fear is not that
>   we are inadequate.
>
> Our deepest fear is that we are
>   powerful beyond measure. . . .
>
> There is nothing enlightened
>   about shrinking so that
>   others won't feel insecure
>   around you. . . .
>
> As we let our light shine,
> We unconsciously give other people
>   permission to do the same.
>
> As we are liberated from our own fears
>   our presence automatically
>   liberates others.

 Liberate yourself and others with the power of your voice.

YOUR LANGUAGE

We clearly understand from the previous chapters that your words are your most powerful tools of creation. The old adage, "The pen is mightier than the sword," is a true one. It is by the words we speak that we effect lasting change in our lives and the lives of those we touch with our words. Chapter 1 introduced the Sapir-Whorf hypothesis as a linguistic mould theory of how society uses language. Our social reality equals the words we think and speak. When you choose your words within the organizational setting, they must always affirm the experience you desire to be having. This is especially true for public speaking experiences.

DON'T MAKE EXCUSES

Too many individuals use what they perceive as their "not so good English" as an excuse to not participate in open discussions. Regional dialects, foreign accents, urban dialects, and others may all become alibis. Let's make an important clarification: someone's English can be deemed good or bad just as an exercise in grammar and syntax, as with any language; however, communication is always appropriate or inappropriate. Learn to communicate comfortably in a variety of settings around different people. Do not be afraid to bring your accent and ethnic or regional dialect to the mix. They represent the beauty of planet diversity. But keep your words simple, concrete, and topic focused. Some individuals are very concerned about their grammar and limited vocabulary. Then do something about it! Read, read, read! Books not only help to improve your vocabulary, they help expand your worldview and understanding of others. Use every opportunity to listen to how words are used in different settings. Build your vocabulary. Take community college English and reading classes as a refresher. Take a speech communication class.

At work you use words, called jargon, that belong exclusively to the setting and your area of expertise. You learn the jargon to get into and play the *expertise game*. Often the more you use and apply the jargon, the more expertise you possess.

Language is always evolving and so should your vocabulary. Choose your words carefully when you speak in public. Make sure you keep your sentences simple, clear, but descriptive. Be sure to avoid or define terminology that may not be familiar to the entire audience. Paint pictures that are easy for people to visualize. Generally you have a time constraint attached to public forums. Learn to present your area of expertise in a variety of time lengths for short or longer presentations. Outlining your subject in 5-, 10-, 20-, and 45-minute increments will help with this. Carefully choose words that will offer the most impact in a succinct manner. Use the following checklist to consider how to choose your words for your public message:

- [ ] Use denotative (dictionary) meanings of words versus connotative (slang) meanings.
- [ ] Use words that are concrete (literal) in meaning versus abstract (figurative).
- [ ] Consider words that translate easily to all your listeners.
- [ ] Keep words and phrasing simple.
- [ ] Make sure you appropriately and expertly use the jargon of your job.
- [ ] Use multicultural references.
- [ ] Be gender aware.
- [ ] Use words that paint a picture and provide color and texture.
- [ ] Use your best volume, diction, and other paralanguage (Chapter 2).

YOUR PUBLIC PRESENTATIONAL STYLE

Delivery and style are also areas of skill and training for the public presenter. There are four different delivery methods that you may use to deliver your message. They are: (1) impromptu,

(2) extemporaneous, (3) manuscript, and (4) memorized. *Impromptu* is basically everyday discourse, unplanned opportunities to contribute to the group on the spur of the moment. *Extemporaneous* is the most frequently used speech method. It involves a researched, outlined, prepared speech using note cards for organization and salient points. Generally the speaker is well acquainted with her message and only uses note cards to keep on track. *Manuscript* speaking entails a printed speech delivered word for word. This is the most difficult of the four methods and is generally used by professionals under time constraints and/or when sharing technical information. *Memorized* speeches are often delivered as short, special-occasion speeches; think of award ceremonies, announcements, after-dinner speeches, and other commemorative occasions. Some individuals, such as actors, have the gift of memorization. Many people shy away from relying on memory, but short memorized speeches at special occasions work best with this format. Most presenters, at one point or another during their career, find themselves using all delivery methods, but generally a given presenter has one method that is most comfortable.

Many prefer *extemporaneous* as their delivery method because it allows the speaker to interact and feed off the audience, and be flexible with their message. Nothing exceeds the role of preparation when you go before an audience. Researching and organizing your speech is just as important as writing a research document. Acquaint yourself with how to outline a speech. It is basically the same process as for an expository composition: central thesis statement and three or more major supporting points (depending on time constraints), all of it shaped into an introduction, body, and conclusion. A simple pattern for a five-minute extemporaneous speech follows:

I. Introduction: Central Thesis
II. Body
   A. Major supporting point
      i. details

B. Major supporting point
   i. details
C. Major supporting point
   i. details

III. Conclusion: Summarize

Your research details should provide supporting points, both in the form of reasoning and evidence, such as relevant statistics. Since you should be speaking on a topic you are well acquainted with, the research should only be a supplement to your professional genius. Choose the method that works best for you, and be flexible depending on the environment and audience.

Finding your individual professional style involves a blending of your verbal, vocal, and visual messages. Too often, novice speakers will stand before their audience not totally synergetic in their delivery. There is a lot of nervous movement, lack of eye contact, weak or unexpressive vocal energy; these patterns diminish the speaker's credibility. Make sure that, when practicing your presentation (and you will practice), you audio- and videotape yourself. See yourself as others see you and it will help you create the visual and vocal image you want to portray. Be aware of your visual message and make sure you feel good about your physical presence. I advise my clients to always "dress up" if they are going to speak in front of a group. Not only does it help you exude confidence to your audience, but YOU feel better about you. Meet with an image consultant who can advise you on colors, hairstyles, clothing styles, and so on. Your professional style should reflect your natural good looks and professional appropriateness (see Application 5.3). And a word of advice: a couple of well-tailored, timeless professional outfits will go much further than less expensive, "what's in," fly-by-night fashions.

Be aware of and practice good diction, volume, pacing, and other nonverbal vocal patterns (paralanguage). Do you feel comfortable with your vocabulary? Do you share enthusiasm in

123

Application 5.3 - Professional Attire

Take an evening to go through your "professional closet." Do you have clothes designated for work that reflect the type of attitude and energy you want to project?

We have all heard of red as the power color. Why? Because someone said so and others agreed, based on the relationship of the color red to our culture. At any rate, it works for some. You can try sporting a tie or a scarf with red in it.

Check out your shoes, your particular style, your colors. Make an honest assessment. Is it time for a new image, a more professional one? A bit of creativity and smart shopping can go a lot further than your pocketbook, if that is a concern.

Ask a trusted friend, colleague, or image consultant for help. Look your professional best!

your voice about your topic? Are you accustomed to varying your inflection, using emphasis and stress, pacing your words in a manner that keeps interest? Are you overly concerned with your accent or dialect? Again, focus on your skills and keep your sentences short, simple, but energetic! Be comfortable with *you* and your unique way of expressing yourself. Think about the professional sports and news people who have made a living off their distinctive voices and looks. Practice words and regional pronunciation that are unfamiliar so that you feel more comfortable in your work setting.

Are you using eye contact that reflects confidence? You must consistently invite each individual in the room to be a part of the discussion. You do this with eye contact. Consistently sweep the room, resting about two to three seconds on each member, or on each section of the audience if the assembly is larger. Watch out for favoring one side of the audience versus the other. Your listeners are very sensitive to this. Eye contact is one of the most important tools of the public speaker.

Do your gestures (kinesics) reflect a high level of comfort with your topic and the audience? Be natural with your gestures. Use your hands and body the same as you would in everyday conversation. Avoid holding on to the lectern (podium) or keeping your hands behind your back. Try not to use repetitive gestures or overuse your hands. Be comfortable and easy with your body movement. Stand tall and firmly plant your feet and move with purpose. Be very conscious of nervous swaying, constant pacing, fidgeting with objects, and leaning on the lectern. You must hone your public communication to reflect your natural, comfortable state of being, one that is nicely polished and confident. Bringing the visual, vocal, and verbal message in sync will achieve this.

YOU AND YOUR AUDIENCE

Understanding your audience and your purpose in speaking is paramount to presentational success. You want to make your points clear and effective to achieve the results you are looking for. Chapter 6 will help you understand the impact of persuasive messages on your audience. At this point what we want to understand is this: regardless of whether your message is informative, persuasive, or entertaining, knowing your audience and knowing the occasion are major contributors to your effectiveness. When we examine our audience, we want to look at:

- demographics
- level of topic understanding
- purpose for attending and listening
- receptivity to speaker and topic

Always inquire, "To whom am I speaking?" Your audience demographics include age, gender, ethnicity, ability, socioeconomic level, religion, group affiliation, education level, and other variables that define the position and attitude of your audience. This attitude directly affects your listeners' receptivity to your message. With this information you must prepare a message that is suitable and effective for the listeners. Think about how you would create a message to relate to your entire audience. You would create a different message about finances for a group of seventh-graders versus a group of AARP members. You would be aware of sociopolitical differences if your audience was very diverse. You may have a different set of quotes and statistics you present to an all-female audience versus one that is gender mixed.

Remember, even when speaking to a small or large group, you are still part of an interpersonal dialogue. You are speaking individually to each listener and meeting them where they are when it comes to their understanding and receptivity to your message. You might create a message that presents quotes from individuals from different cultures you want to acquaint yourself with, or investigate philosophies that are not so congruent with your way of thinking. You may need to explore a socioeconomic awareness of how your topic impacts people's financial reality. Do your homework to know who is at the meeting and what messages would best inspire their interest. What are the roles and outcomes people seek? The organizational culture will provide clear messages of who your audience is and how to communicate with them. Demographics play a major role in your achieving your goal to impact your listeners.

Speaking in front of a group requires that you pay special attention to the purpose of your speech! Are you informing or persuading? These are the two speaking activities you will be switching between during your entire workday. On occasion, you may get in a bit of humor. Make sure you're on the same page as your audience by thinking about their knowledge level regarding your topic. Should you come in at the ABCs, or is the audience intermediate, even advanced? Make sure you are knowledgeable about your audience's level and your ability to meet their needs. You should always, always only present a topic you feel very confident about. Silence can be golden.

If you are anything like most members of an organization, when called to participate in a meeting you wish you were anyplace else. The degree to which your listeners want to be a part of the audience is also the degree to which you can expect their attention and receptiveness. Know the purpose of your participants' attendance. Review the following audience checklist:

☐ Are they being mandated to attend professional development or monthly department meeting?

☐ Is it a special occasion and a time to relax and enjoy the fruits of the group's labor?

☐ Is a hot-button issue being dealt with?

☐ Are opposing viewpoints present?

☐ Are you the deliverer of bad news?

☐ How welcome are you as a speaker?

☐ Do you know the members of the group?

☐ How do they respond to you in the workplace?

☐ What is your level of speaker credibility?

☐ How do people in your own department relate to you; how about people elsewhere in the organization?

These are vital questions to ask as you prepare yourself and your message. Always remember that knowing your audience and knowing the occasion are vital ingredients to public speaking success. They provide the foundation for your message and your approach to public presentational success.

THE ART OF IMPROMPTU/CONVERSATIONAL SPEAKING

Have you ever been in a meeting or at an office party and felt out of place? No matter how cool, calm, and collected you thought you were, there was another voice in the back of your head screaming loudly for you to run for cover! Many say they often feel as if they suffered from the proverbial "foot in mouth" when they try and engage in small talk. What is the problem, you wonder? Why can't you come off as confident and composed as Bill What's-his-name? You know the one. When he opens his mouth his teeth sparkle and charisma oozes from his lips. Yeah, that one.

Small talk and/or impromptu communication is an area of speaking that everyone has to take part in. There is an endless stream of communication experiences in the workplace including department meetings, evaluations, interviews, board meetings, and workshops, all of them requiring you to function as a confident and ready impromptu speaker. The apprehension I hear most often concerning impromptu speaking is "I don't have anything interesting to say!" This may be so. Most individuals live very insular lives and are generally interested only in issues that affect them personally. Go back to Jill's story, situation #5. Remember her encounter with David and how she had so much she wanted to say but just could not formulate her words. She missed a good opportunity to get her point across. How effective can our companies be when filled with people who find it so hard to have conversations with one another? Ask questions. Be inquisitive.

 In order to be a good conversationalist, you must be aware, open, and positively inquisitive.

A good conversationalist is aware of the things happening around him and beyond him. I meet so many people who are extremely myopic—they are focused only on themselves. If something does not affect them directly, they are not interested. Many situations and people become invisible to them, even those within the personal and social sphere. But, interestingly, they vicariously relish the experiences of distant tabloid stars. What they truly value shows in their awareness. When trying to engage them in community news, in civic concerns, they are clueless. These same people may also easily overlook the "community news" of the workplace. They are often too concerned with their next promotion. An awareness of your surrounding community, organizational news, and concerns can go a long way to engaging coworkers, neighbors, and civic leaders in conversation when needful and desirable.

Being open is the key to an extraordinary life. When we are open, we learn so much from others.

You cannot teach yourself anything new. All knowledge comes from outside in.

This is why listening is an important ingredient in the art of conversation. In order to listen, you have to be open. Many good conversationalists engage in communication that is a constant give-and-take, listening to the other speaker and creating discussion around her discussion. Reading a variety of materials and learning about a variety of world experiences are ways you can engage in openness that supports your conversation with others. No one is an expert on everything, or even most things. But people who are adept and comfortable with small talk can say a little about a lot. Be open and you will have a lot of interesting things to say. When you encounter perspectives in the workplace that do not mirror your own, listen respectfully and understand two important points:

1. There are always two messages—the one you send and the one they receive.
2. There is always more than one way to look at and solve any problem.

Try to acquaint yourself with the members of your department/division and their responsibilities. This is not only a good idea to help members extend mutual respect for one another, but it is also good career sense. Branch out beyond your area, meet and learn from others in the organization. Be aware of everything it takes for the organization to run smoothly and cooperatively. Being open to other points of view and experiences in the workplace is a wonderful tool for advancement and cohesion.

Having a healthy sense of inquisitiveness is important. The explorer in you should be a regular visitor to the outside world. I want to reiterate the word "healthy." We live in a society of distraction. We live in a culture where "reality TV" has taken voyeurism to an all-time high! As a culture, we love to spy into the lives of others. It appears to be America's favorite pastime, from *Survivor* to *The Apprentice*. This creates a false connection and genuine indifference to REAL people! So, by "healthy," I do not mean the curiosity people have for talk-show gossip, but a real connection with the people you work with and live with every day. You should have a healthy interest in the global marketplace you compete in! Awareness, openness, and healthy curiosity are the keys to being a good conversationalist.

Additionally, BE PREPARED! Impromptu opportunities to speak at work can come at a moment's notice. If you have the slightest hint or inclination that you may be required to contribute, be ready! Read the department memos and materials on the topics being discussed at the meeting. Talk with colleagues about the issues and probable solutions. Again, do your homework and be prepared when you go into the meeting. Volunteer for opportunities to represent your division. Employ the tools of confidence and composure when you speak. Do not talk yourself out of contributing. Find your voice to express and support your contribution to the group discussion. You are as valuable to the organization as your ability to articulate your contribution and worth!

Public speaking can propel your professional career to new heights! Review the chapter tips often, but especially when you have to present a report, attend an office social, participate in a workshop, or simply join in a lunchroom discussion. Being prepared and confident to use your voice in any circumstance you desire is a skill most people do not have. But the ones that do are the ones climbing the corporate ladder with speed!

This step and the next have a close connection. The mass messages and persuasive appeals we constantly receive and give create the platform from which we often speak. Get ready to explore the "art" of persuasion.

Q & A Public Communication

Dear PS,

Q: I am often asked to speak for my department at the quarterly meetings. I am terrified every time! I have taken a couple of public speaking classes and even joined Toastmasters for a short while. I did great in the classes, but I just can't shake the jitters when speaking at work.

A: This is not uncommon. Many people find it easier to address "anonymous," nonjudgmental audiences than they do their colleagues. Greater ease takes time and it takes a level of self-confidence that can penetrate the illusion of judgment and approval. After preparing and practicing your delivery, engage in psychological preparation. See yourself cool, calm, and collected. Remember, FEAR is False Evidence Appearing Real! Prepare, visualize, and talk yourself into success!

Q: I grew up with a speech impediment. I had a bad lisp as a child, but a speech pathologist helped me to reduce it to be almost inaudible. Unfortunately, when I have to speak in public, it returns! I use the exercises I was given as a child, but they do not seem to help when I am front and center.

A: Nervousness is normal. It is your anxiety that is bringing forward your old speaking habits. When you practice your speech, pay close attention to the words you are prone to lisp. Slow down and over-enunciate these words during practice, over and over again. In addition, use visual imaging to see and hear yourself effortlessly producing the words. If speaking is very important to your role at work, think about going back to a speech specialist for additional support. Try very hard to have the same level of control and intimacy in your public presentations as you do in your private ones, so you can take away the "public" focus and relax.

Q: I often forget what I am going to talk about when it's my turn at the meeting.

A: You are a prime candidate for extemporaneous delivery. Always prepare a brief outline on 3 x 5 cards and take them with you. Commit as much of the info as possible to memory, but do not be afraid to use the cards for support.

Q: I tend to look at one side of the audience when speaking. I have even had audience members come and say they felt left out, but I can't seem to kick the habit.

A: Most speakers are drawn to the side of the audience that corresponds to their most dominant side, which is usually the speaker's right. Whichever side you prefer, look for something on the neglected side that catches your interest, be it a person or thing, and do so as soon as you enter the setting where you will give your talk. Connect with this anchor in a way that encourages you to look for it during your speech. Broaden your eye contact from that spot into the entire area. Remember your manners and include everyone in the conversation you are having. Have the consciousness of inclusiveness and it will remind you to invite everyone to the table.

Q: I have been asked to present at the regional conference in the place of my manager, who cannot attend. I do not think I can do it, but I am afraid to back out.

A: First and foremost: if you think you cannot do it, you are right! You cannot achieve what you do not believe. So go back to Chapter 1 and spend some time monitoring your beliefs about yourself and the changes you need to make for your own personal and professional success. If it is a matter of not having the knowledge level, never let anyone force you to do what you know you are not prepared to do well. If it's a matter of a bit of homework, then get at it and dare yourself to meet the challenge. Determine if you have enough time to do so; if not, put forth the name of a qualified colleague and prepare yourself for the next opportunity.

Mass Communication

. . . new technology cannot be a substitute for human values . . .

—-Neil Postman, *Amusing Ourselves to Death*

INFLUENCING THE MASSES

Mass Communication is *the multiple message system that connects members of a society or group to one another by means of public communication for the purpose of maintaining cultural values, norms, attitudes, and beliefs.* In short, it is a society's means of propaganda. Through the airwaves, billboards, newspapers, magazines, tabloids, the Internet, and other forms of Mass Communication, we all consistently receive the worldview or perspective of the dominant culture. In the United States, as in much of the Western world, that dominant worldview is based on a Eurocentric, patriarchal system. From this viewpoint, we obtain a perspective of information designed to create an agreed-upon awareness of societal expectations. Through the process of diffusion, a blending or sharing of cultural experiences, we experience the messages of co-cultures as they bring their perspective to the table. So, whereas the majority of mass messages are framed from the dominant cultural perspective, the heterogeneous makeup of the culture creates room for differing points of view.

It is through the channels of Mass Communication that we consume a variety of societal messages. The question examined during the sixth step of effective communication is how these messages affect your life. How susceptible are you to the pervasiveness of the manipulation all around you? Do these messages impact the quality of your work life? Are you aware that at the root of all Mass Communication is the objective of getting you to do one of three things? Read on.

PERSUASION IS ABOUT PERSPECTIVE

Mass Communication offers us instruction about our society and the world around us; entertainment based on the cultural mores we find amusing; viewpoints that allow us to experience the contradictions in how differing cultures see the world; standards of success and beauty and their acquisition; and of course the propaganda that reinforces the culture's specific worldview. There are many models that exist to explain the occurrence of Mass Communication. They can pretty much be simplified to a source sending a message through a specific channel to encourage a particular outcome. In their work *The People's Choice*, Lazarsfeld, Berelson, and Gaudet describe a three-step approach, *with source, receivers,* and *opinion leaders* all involved in the cyclical sharing of mass messages. *Opinion leaders* are responsible for sharing their perspective on the issues we face as a society. *Gatekeepers* basically serve the same function and filter the messages we receive, based on a number of determinants but usually those that advance the aim of the dominant source. All of this adds up to a pretty controlled environment of mass messages that are tailored to keep the dominant perspective in charge. Think about this dynamic in relation to the organizational environment. How is the mission of the organization consistently reinforced? Who is the source? Who are the gatekeepers? It should be clear that, as in other social or professional settings, all organizations use mass and persuasive appeals to maintain the dominant viewpoint. Who controls the message? I learned very early:

 "He who controls the words, controls everything."

I am reminded of a commercial I saw on Italian television during a visit in the fall of 2003. There was no spoken dialogue, but the music was haunting and the images showed a variety of people engaged in some form of communication, such as reading a newspaper, reading directional signs while driving, reading a billboard, and playing from sheet music. The thing that was so unique about the ad was that all the messages on the various mediums had been erased, which you could see when there was a close-up. All the papers, signs, and billboards were blank. The people were looking at nothing. The commercial was in black and white, which added to the haunting quality. At the end of the ad, we saw a group of children sitting together and all of a sudden there was a rush of color and the sound of laughter.

It was a very effective ad about the dangers of censorship. The history of the world is replete with examples of the enormity of the power of the word to effect change, more so than any other tool of change. We remember and still witness the propaganda of Nazi Germany, the word power of the abolition and suffragists' movements, peace talk efforts between Israel and

Palestine, the Civil Rights Movement, the Gay Rights Movement, Global AIDS Awareness, the Green Movement, groups such as Amnesty International, racial reconciliation talks in South Africa, and the list goes on and on of groups coming together to effect change with their voices.

Mass Communication affords us the opportunity to get the word out and enlist the minds of others to join us in our causes. The cause might be "help my business grow by buying my product" or "vote for me and I will be your voice for change." Whatever the cause, the power of the word is unparalleled in its ability to move the masses to act! How does this type of persuasion play a role in your decision making? What are the messages being dumped into your business *lake* on a daily basis: competition, praise, a raise, rivalry, downsizing, restructuring, greed, co-opetition? There are a number of factors that affect the way you ingest the propaganda being served up. Are you a part of the power elite? Are you a member of a marginalized group, such as those who experience disabilities? Are you 25 or 55 years old? Are you financially solvent or dependent, living paycheck to paycheck? In a male-dominated work culture, are you male or female?

All of these factors and hundreds more affect the way you are sent workplace messages and the way you receive them. Why are we susceptible to the persuasive messages of our social and professional environments? The same need for approval that drives our social needs also drives our professional needs. We all want to feel vital, appreciated for our perceived genius. Ultimately, the vast majority thrives to "have it all" in an endless effort to be the one with the "most toys."

ARE YOU A WALKING BILLBOARD?

The studies on the effects of Mass Communication can be traced back to pioneers such as Neil Postman's, *Amusing Ourselves to Death*. The workplace is a microcosm of the social macrocosm.

The mass messages that pervade our social environment, messages designed to set up the "pecking order" of life, are also prevalent in our smaller work cultures. Look at the way our mass media reflects our culture at large. Sitcoms such as *The Simpsons, South Park,* and many others have been blamed for the demise of respect and caring within the family unit. Video games have been challenged for their violent nature and what is perceived as resultant aggressive behavior, mainly in young males. Crime shows such as *Cops* and the *Lock Up* series are reality television shows that ask us to tune into the worst side of human nature as well as become voyeurs in an increasingly fear-based society. Daytime talk shows too often give a platform to the worst character traits. And to top it all off, we are consistently inundated with commercials persuading us to consume the latest time-saving gadget, new toy, or luxury car. The distractions are endless. If anything, they generally complicate things by providing an endless sea of perspectives and choices tumbling from out of other people's movies. Depending on your ability to exercise mind over matter, you are more or less susceptible to the outside influences of the daily propaganda of your environment. It's like the movie *The Matrix.* Most people are plugged into a world of endless illusions and distractions, and do not want to be unplugged. Take a look at the statistics below.

Television Habits

I. Family Life

Percentage of households that possess at least one television: 99

Number of hours of TV watched annually by Americans: 250 billion

II. Children

Number of minutes per week that parents spend in meaningful conversation with their children: 3.5

Number of minutes per week that the average child watches television: 1,680

III. Violence

Number of murders seen on TV by the time an average child finishes elementary school: 8,000

Number of violent acts seen on TV by age 18: 200,000

IV. Commercialism

Number of 30-second TV commercials seen in a year by an average child: 20,000

Number of TV commercials seen by the average person by age 65: 2 million

Compiled by TV-Free America,
www.csun.edu/science/health/docs/tv&health.html#tv_stats

Does art mirror life or life mirror art? *Who Wants to Marry a Millionaire?* counsel with *Dr. Phil* but still hopelessly end up in *Divorce Court?* How many of us feel that our lives are a game of *Jeopardy* where we must constantly play *Survivor* due to all the *Fear Factor?* Whose life movie are you starring in? How many of these mindless mass signals are being added to your lake? How much does what you are receiving determine how you see and feel about yourself? Persuasion is an art that has been mastered by the manipulators of communication. We sometimes call them producers, directors, advertising executives, con men, charlatans, editors, lawyers, salespeople, and a host of other titles given to those who have mastered the art of persuasive communication. Many individuals "create" themselves as a collage of images they receive through mass media (see Figure 6.1).

PERSUASION AND THE WORLD OF WORK

As in the macrocosm, so in the smaller world of work. Think about the amount of information disseminated through formal

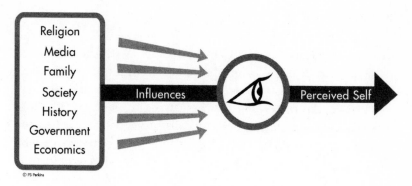

Religion
Media
Family
Society
History
Government
Economics

Influences

Perceived Self

© PS Perkins

Figure 6.1 Perceived Self-Socialization

and informal networks, as discussed in Chapter 4. How many e-mails, memos, briefs, reports, and other documents come across your desk or computer on a daily basis designed to advance the imperative of the organizational mission? Mandate after mandate is put forth by the "source" in its effort to make sure YOU are functioning in the manner that progresses the organizational agenda.

This is the function of communications in the workplace. If you are working in an environment where the organizational mission and culture support your individual contribution in a manner that allows you to "own" the organizational vision, then these communications should foster satisfaction and success as you follow them. For you, the directives are clear and the culture is functioning at a high level of inclusion and productivity that you feel valued in. You have a part in creating the messages that advance the organizational goal. The "propaganda" has a positive effect on the communication climate. Those who do not feel valued and are working in an organizational environment that they find toxic will also consider corporate communications to be lacking in value, discriminatory, and out of sync with their understanding of "what's wrong."

JILL'S DAY

We can see Jill experiencing this problem. With the change in management, she no longer felt that her opinion was valued. This immediately gave rise to fault finding with the directive concerning implementing the new tracking strategy in situation #6. She vehemently defended the "old way" and resisted the mandate to replace the old system. Her reaction can be seen from a variety of perspectives. Jill and other *gatekeepers* want their expert opinions valued before implementing such changes. Jill felt devalued and disrespected. On the other end, the *source* from which the mandate flows feels persuaded that this is the immediate course of action to take for the good of the organization. There was no consideration of the manner in which the new message should be infused into the organization and how to transition workers to the new way of handling things. This could be a costly decision. Persuasion is the tool used by the message creators to influence the receivers to act as desired (see Application 6.1). The importance of the

Application 6.1 - Persuasive Messages

Personal Inventory

Make a personal inventory for a day or even a week, if you can stay focused. Take note of the number and types of persuasive messages you receive on a daily basis at work. Who is asking what of you?

What methods are they using—speaker credibility (the supervisor), desires (a raise), or logic (this is why it must be done this way)? How are you most easily persuaded?

target audience cannot be overlooked. For our purposes, the target audience is those members of the organizational culture who must respond with action. Jill did not respond positively to the persuasive message.

USING PERSUASION AS A TOOL OF INFLUENCE

Attitudes based on values and beliefs can be altered as individuals come in contact with influences that alter their beliefs. Do you believe the same things today as you did when you were a child—Santa Claus, the Easter bunny, a knight in shining armor? No, you do not. You are constantly evolving in your attitudes, as well as holding fast to those deep values that define how you see yourself and your place in the world. During your professional career, you will be presenting countless persuasive messages to your target audience—the members of your organization. These messages will be designed to motivate, convince, or actuate.

Your audience may agree with your message, be neutral to the message, or be strongly opposed to the message. Your aim with those who agree will be to maintain or strengthen their current level of support. Those who are neutral to your message will need to be convinced that your position is a benefit to them and the organization. There are still others that you will want to move to action. They will need to not only agree with your message but also put that message into action. Sometimes this is a simple matter of gentle persuasion, and sometimes this is a matter of force or coercion. It is important that you understand where the members of your target audience stand concerning your message. This will determine what strategies you should use to affect your audience and ensure their support of your message. In order to understand this, you must be aware of the tools of manipulation used to effect change in yourself and others (see Figure 6.2).

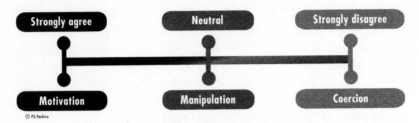

Figure 6.2 Spectrum of Influence

AS SIMPLE AS ONE, TWO, THREE

The masters of manipulation, the spin doctors of propaganda, have reduced our reasons and our ways to persuade down to a simple but all-encompassing formula. There are basically three (3) reasons to persuade and three (3) ways to do it. First is the *why*. Persuasive messages have as their *reason,* or goal, to: (1) take some type of action, (2) change a strong attitude or belief, or (3) motivate you to maintain a certain belief or weaken a current belief. What about the attitude, values, and beliefs you hold now? Think of the professional decisions you have made over the years. What actions have you taken? What beliefs have gotten you to this point?

- Do you have a college degree?
- Did you attend a trade school or go straight to work after high school, if you finished? What is your chosen profession?
- Did your work choose you or did you choose it?
- Were you talked out of your dream career?
- Are you happy with the professional decisions you have made?

All the answers to these questions are based on your individual socialization and the messages you integrated, mainly during adolescence and early adulthood.

144

There are three (3) basic *ways* to persuade: (1) facts and reasoning (logic), (2) speaker credibility (ethics), and/or (3) appealing to some basic emotion, need, want, or desire (emotions). Aristotle introduced these ways or methods as *proofs:* logical proof as Logos, ethical proof as ethos, and emotional proof as pathos. After being introduced by Aristotle more than 2,000 years ago, these proofs still hold up as the fundamental persuasive appeals.

Evidence and reasoning, or *Logos,* is the persuasive appeal we experience most in settings where evidence and reasoning are required to prove and validate results. In school, we are taught to engage in critical thinking and to use reasoning to come to conclusions that can be supported. We learn various types of reasoning methods including deductive, inductive, analogical and causal reasoning. We are governed by laws that use the logic of cause and effect to create order and discipline. Laws concerning driving under the influence of alcohol are good examples of this. We experience Logos when we are persuaded concerning scientific discoveries, health information, rules governing societal conditions, educational paradigms, and other spheres where logic is the standard of accountability. Remember when the Surgeon General, C. Everett Koop, gave his dire warnings concerning the addiction and health risks of cigarette smoking, how he provided proofs of the dangers. Thousands, possibly millions were persuaded to quit! There were other types of appeals used to reach individuals from a more emotional appeal such as the appeals from the Marlboro Man (who had experienced the dangers firsthand). However, it continues to be the evidence and reasoning of health information that convinces millions to kick or not start the habit. Examine the continuing discussions concerning the origin of human life and the arguments of evolution versus creationism. We can examine many norms, rules, traditions, and laws that have been exercised by cultures based on the logical proofs used to persuade the masses. Our organizations are often subject to this type of persuasion, with evidence put forth to support one model versus another. Many of us require the proof of logic before feeling assured that a particular method is the best model of implementation.

Speaker credibility, or ethos, is the appeal put forth to individuals who are most influenced by what others think and say. Often this appeal is used to sell a product or idea that is endorsed by a celebrity or recognized spokesperson. Think of all the celebrity endorsements for cars, footgear, perfumes, household products, financial investments, and the list goes on. Many people are more easily influenced by what others say than by what they themselves think. Think of household names, from Alan Greenspan, the ex-chairman of the Federal Reserve, to Oprah Winfrey, global media mogul, and of the enormous impact these individuals can have on our social, political, and economic affairs with just a word! Who were the individuals in our lives to first teach us about speaker credibility? They were our parents and caretakers. Within the structure of a family, whatever its makeup, we first learned about speaker credibility. Each of us, depending on our early relationship with those in authority, have created for ourselves a certain perception of how we see, feel, and deal with those who have authority over us. For some, the early years were filled with respect, admiration, and good judgment from those we afforded speaker credibility. Their ethics were in line with their authority. Unfortunately, many growing up were not introduced to speaker credibility in a manner that created trust and respect. They suffered or were poorly guided by those in charge. Those early experiences definitely affect how they experience authority in their lives now.

When we examine the organizational hierarchy, we experience the power of speaker credibility. The "Y pattern" of formal communications has as its model the hierarchy of credibility. Under the organizational framework, this equates to power. Things happen in the organization based on the word of those who are in charge. Titles such as CEO, CFO, COO, president, chairperson of the board, founder, and other labels attest to the importance of credibility as a persuasive force within the organization. We all seek speaker credibility within our workplaces (see Application 6.2). We want to be recognized as the authority or expert in our field. We want to be respected, and when we speak we want people to listen! This drive to be acknowledged and given credit is basic to human vitality, and most of us spend our lives seeking it through interpersonal relationships and professional pursuits.

Emotional appeal, or *pathos,* is a persuasive tool used to effect change by appeals to needs, wants, and desires. There are entire industries that survive based on the persuasive power of emotional appeals, often labeled fear "appeals." Ponder the mass messages we receive on a daily basis that are couched in fear, in the need for acceptance or approval, in love, sympathy or empathy, or that play to our basic survival needs. Many individuals are led to make choices based on how they *feel.* Countless ads and infomercials play on our sentiments to join them in the cause of alleviating hunger, saving the whales, stopping global warming, and staying forever young. Just think about the multibillon-dollar industry of cosmetic surgery. What societal messages are encouraging the obsession with plastic surgery, Botox, fitness gyms, diet crazes, and weight-reduction procedures? Think about the level of the fear appeals that have made

Application 6.2 - Your Professional Credibility

During your next department meeting with coworkers, take a silent inventory of your speaker credibility.

Pay attention to how the members of the group respond to your input. Are they attentive? Are the nonverbal cues responsive? Do you feel that your input is being taken seriously? Does your contribution provoke serious conversation?

You may want to expand this to a day or a workweek, paying close attention to HOW individuals at work are responding to your input. What steps can you take to increase your credibility?

security services one of the fastest-growing industries in the world. Indeed, many individuals are making choices daily based on the emotional appeals they are bombarded with.

How good are you at recognizing emotional appeals in the workplace? How often do you and your colleagues feel the stress and fear of a looming deadline? What creates that fear? Is it the thought that if you do not meet the deadline, your position will be adversely affected and you might possibly lose your job? How about the colleague who is constantly pleading to be bailed out of some problem created by poor decision making? With the current climate of globalization and the powerful global marketplace, many workers feel the ever tightening grip of performing at a level that assures them job security. Many organizations are going through restructuring and downsizing, which turn into fear factors for workers who could be adversely affected by the changes. Promotions, appraisals, evaluations, and other forms of judgment all conjure up for most the emotional connection to our self-worth or our value to the organization.

PERSUASIVE MESSAGES AND YOU

Not only are we the target of persuasive appeals, but we also spend our lives influencing others to see things our way. We are all creatures seeking to persuade others to join us in our dream or validate our reality. Generally, the tactics you used as a child to get the things you wanted are the same tactics you use as an adult. Did you throw tantrums, hold your breath, use physical force, cry and pout, refuse to eat? Use deceit or charm and wit? Most likely, what you thought worked then is what you continue to use now. And you attract others to you who are easily influenced by these methods, or else they do not play the game. Notice the manner you seek to effect change in the workplace. Do you tend to gather all the evidence first and approach the problem logically, or use your influence power to "do as I say"? When faced with conflict, do you tend to react emotionally? Are you the coworker who is always going to management with concerns about your department, seeking their credibility to validate your position? We tend to use the same tactics in our professional arenas as we do in our personal arenas, to the extent that we can get away with it.

Each of us is more likely to be persuaded by one tactic or type of persuasion than another. Which type of persuasive appeal is most effective in getting you to act? Are you the "show me in black and white" type? No one's going to pull anything over on you. You always read the fine print. (But *who* is writing the fine print?) Are you the type who is always looking to a charismatic voice to show you the way? The boss says jump, and you say, "How high?" Or are you the type easily persuaded by the fear of rejection or the need for affection? One more surgical tuck and you'll be just fine. Abraham Maslow's *hierarchy of needs* theorizes that once our basic needs are taken care of, we can all ascend to the pinnacle of *self-actualization.* So the world is full of people at one end or the other of the pyramid; unfortunately, most are at the bottom. There are those who can think of nothing but where their next meal is coming from, and those who think of nothing but how to obtain the next level of their professional success. What drives and motivates us to make the professional choices we have made, and the choice whether to maintain or change? The prostitute, the political candidate, the teacher, the nun, the conservationist, the activist, the musician, the drug dealer—all starring in their own version of a life movie they have created. Many of us have chosen our life-work based on one of these appeals. Many have chosen a profession because of the financial security it offers. There are those who feel they have sacrificed financial wealth for professions that offer greater contributions to society, such as teaching or nursing. There are those working in a given field only because their parents would not have it any other way. Yes, our professional decisions, just like our personal decisions, are definitely influenced by persuasion, sometimes to our benefit and sometimes to our harm. We are easily persuaded by messages that change the course of our lives, sometimes on a daily basis. It is important that we each take responsibility for the personal and professional choices we are making, recognizing the pervasive onslaught of *other people's stuff* in the attempt to encourage us to live otherwise—outside of our own truth and authenticity.

Where are you in the quest for self-actualization? Are you truly on the path of self-discovery?

Most individuals use and experience a combination of persuasive tools to effect change or action in others. If you are in a leadership position, there may be times when you need facts and data to make the decisions that affect your department's fiscal needs. There may be times when you will present an emotional appeal to stay the course and support a goal that may be taking longer than most envisioned. There may be times where your leadership position demands that you take control and mandate a certain line of action that others find difficult to understand. Mastering persuasive appeals requires that you learn to use all of them, depending on the audience and the desired outcome.

Regardless of your level of susceptibility to the never-ending bombardment of mass messages, they are an integral part of your daily decision making. We all need to be more vigilant, exercising our critical thinking skills to discern truth from fiction relative to our own life movies. If you *unplugged* yourself, what would be the result? What would remain of your dream if you took away all the outside influences of Mass Communication? What would you believe in? What would you aspire to be? Would you make the same decisions professionally if influences had not steered you in a certain way?

The mass messages that persuade all of us daily in our personal and professional lives influence current and future decisions. The well-informed, critically thinking employee and consumer maneuvers through the never-ending onslaught of these persuasive appeals. By recognizing and utilizing the three reasons and three ways, you put yourself in the driver's seat of making choices that positively affect your career.

As we ready ourselves to ascend the final step of the Communication Staircase, reflect upon the inside-out journey you have taken thus far. The previous six steps of communication effectiveness support the seventh step that is so vital to the global workforce we are increasingly encountering—Intercultural Communication.

Q & A Mass Communication

Dear PS,

Q: My coworker is always trying to convince members in our department that his ideas concerning saving the department money are the best way for us to go. The problem is he never presents any concrete evidence that his plans will work. He feels that his seniority should be the determining factor in allowing his ideas to move forward.

A: Your colleague is one of millions who consider that their credibility should be enough, but as this chapter reveals, not every persuasive appeal works for everyone or for every situation. Share with your colleague the need to support his ideas with evidence and reasoning. Help him to understand that, though members of the department respect his seniority, the determination to implement a certain line of action must be based on facts that will support the outcome the department needs.

Q: My boss is always sending out these motivational messages to "start the day with a positive attitude" or saying "one helping hand can change the world." While I appreciate his good nature and positive attitude, I just don't see how all this feel-good stuff helps advance our department objective!

A: Classical models of organizational leadership focus on bottom-line results, as opposed to models that take into account the emotional health of its employees. Most research states that productive work environments combine both models. My advice would be to be grateful for a work environment that fosters employee mental and emotional health.

Q: I tend to be easily influenced by others at work. It's almost like I am afraid to have my own opinion. I also noticed that I am not taken very seriously at work; my career is stalled. How can I change all this?

A: The first step has already been taken. You recognize the need to have your own opinion! Carefully reread Chapter 1 to examine the personal, inner issues that have taken away your ability to think and speak for yourself. Nothing can take the place of understanding why you have given away your voice. Secondly, review the information in this chapter to recognize the ways in which you are easily persuaded. It sounds as if you value the credibility of others more than you do your own. Once you learn to value your own voice, you will not depend on the voice of others.

Q: You discuss the ability of people to change, but I often meet individuals at work who appear unmovable. They just don't want to progress. How do you get through to people like that?

A: Contrary to popular belief, not all change is good. Some people are resistant because they do not see the merit in every newfangled application. As the saying goes, "If it ain't broke, don't fix it!" However, there are times when progress is good and a sound case can be provided to substantiate its merit. This is often what is needed for those who don't want to "fix" what they do not consider "broke." Gather the evidence and provide sound reasoning to support the case for change. Review the information in Chapters 3 and 4 on conflict management and approach your target audience with supportive communication, respect, empathy, and sound reasoning.

Q: I can't seem to convince my boss that I should get a raise! It has been three years since my last raise and all my reviews have been excellent. Every time I approach her about a raise, she says now is not the time to talk about it! I am getting pretty frustrated.

A: Your frustration is understandable, IF you are sure that this is something you are experiencing in isolation from the rest of your coworkers. Are others getting raises and promotions? Are you sure it is not an organization-wide fiscal issue? If you know that others are advancing, then you need to look at the approach you are taking. Discuss the matter with a colleague you trust and who is making advancement. Ask for a candid assessment of what is stalling your advancement. Maybe your appeal is too emotional, as opposed to evidence based. Maybe you could use the support of allies who have the ear of your boss and can add a bit of credibility to your request. Do your homework and plan your persuasive strategy!

Intercultural Communication

"I imagine one of the reasons people cling to their hates so stubbornly is because they sense, once hate is gone, that they will be forced to deal with pain."

—James Baldwin, *Notes of a Native Son*

WE CAN ALL GET ALONG!

The highest art and science of Human Communication is *Intercultural Communication*. This step is a culmination of all the communication skills and knowledge we have discussed in this book thus far. Arriving at this step means that you have traveled up the Communication Staircase, acquiring knowledge and skills that have prepared you to confidently and comfortably communicate across cultures. Intercultural Communication is *communication between individuals or groups from different cultural*

155

backgrounds whose diversity of symbol systems and cultural perspectives influences the communication exchange. It is also referred to as *cross-cultural communication.* We use the word "culture" in its broadest definition to encompass people who share values, attitudes, beliefs, customs, and a symbol system that differentiates them from other groups. This includes but is not limited to religion, sex, gender, age, disability, ethnicity, class, and other groupings that can be distinguished as a culture. Intercultural Communication is a specialized arena of communication founded by the anthropologist Edward T. Hall. His early works included intense sociocultural studies of various cultural groups, including the Hopi Indians, and of the importance language had in creation of their *social reality.* Individuals who are high functioning in the area of cross-cultural communication have successfully navigated the Communication Staircase from the first step to the seventh step (see Figure 7.1). They are comfortable with who they are and have no need to negate the existence of others or the right of others to have a different point of view. They understand that perception is personal. Think of the value of this understanding within the organizational culture. How productive and progressive to have an organization that is filled with individuals functioning at healthy levels of self-worth and inclusion.

WHAT MAKES US UNIQUE

The term *enculturation* refers to the process of socialization experienced by a collective group of people for the purpose of maintaining an agreed-upon worldview of values, attitudes, and beliefs within a common symbol system. This is how we derive culture. Co-cultures exist under the umbrella of the dominant culture but have a different type of enculturation process, due to their unique experience within the dominant culture. Examples would be people who are physically chal-

Figure 7.1 Intercultural Communication

lenged, or ethnic groups such as Native Americans. These groups and many others have experienced what is termed *acculturation,* which is the process of being socialized into the dominant culture while maintaining identity and fluidity within their own. Through the process of enculturation, there is a layering of identity that creates our cultural, sociocultural, and psychocultural selves (see Figure 7.2). It is the totality of the individual that we interact with and create relationships with, not just that aspect which is familiar to us (say, a common language). Our organizations include individuals who are constantly experiencing acculturation through their contact with the dominant culture. The aim is for varying perspectives to come together to help the organization meet its objectives and goals. The applied tools of Intercultural Communication can

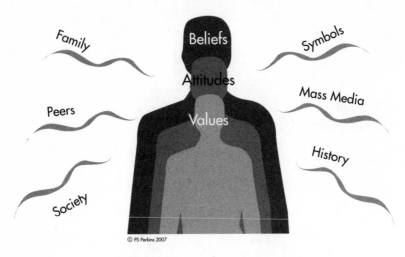

Figure 7.2 Enculturation Process

make this happen for any institution dedicated to inclusion and innovation.

Intercultural Communication helps us examine how the individual fits into the present global community, into global business, the global economy, global concerns, and global mass communication. Why do we need instruction in cross-cultural communication? Because people are unique. Each of us experiences life and sees things differently. It is the denial of these differences that continues to cause the strife that exists between us. Yes, we are more similar than we are different. But the differences in some cases are so profound, on the basic level of existence, that it is unwise to try and continue to ignore them. Instead we should acknowledge and celebrate them. Scoffers will say that those of us who focus on *differences* are just making it harder for everyone to get along. These dissenters are the true separatists, the true elitists. Very often, when you really question their "color-blind" philosophies, what they are saying loud and clear is "Why can't everyone be like me!?" Because, just as soon as they witness some eating ritual, deities worship, tradition, or custom unlike their own, they are the first to cry, "Pagan, barbaric, disgusting!" We share the same planet, breath the same air, need the same water, want the same peace, and generally desire the same freedoms—for our own! We look through the lens of *ethnocentrism*, thinking that our way is the best way. In this seventh and final step, we look inward to ascend upward in our ability to positively affect all people we encounter within our diverse organizations and the global marketplace.

WE ARE ALL PREJUDICED!

That is to say, we all have preferences. Some prefer Coke or to have their coffee black versus with cream. Some prefer to date exclusively within their ethnic circles; others enjoy a broad variety of dating choices. All of these *prejudices* are personal and private choices each individual deserves to make. But, as with all attitudes, prejudice can have extremes, and it is the extremes that become detrimental to an organization that must function as a unit. Examine Figure 7.3 to see the spectrum of how an individual may engage in prejudiced behavior.

Ethnocentrism is the belief that your cultural group is superior, better than others. However, being ethnocentric can mean you have a healthy pride in your cultural heritage and national identity. *Bigotry* is the face shown by extreme ethnocentrism as

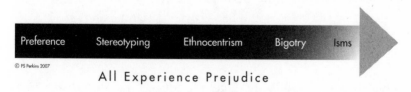

© PS Perkins 2007

All Experience Prejudice

Figure 7.3 Spectrum of Prejudice

it surfaces in your daily interactions, when you compare yourself with others. *Stereotypes* are generalizations formed out of prejudice and applied in a sweeping manner, without accurate evidence. *Isms* are the resultant actions that oppress others simply because the people are different: ageism, racism, sexism, homophobism, and the like. This extreme denotes the power to alter the reality of the person or group being oppressed. This is why it is often hard for a "minority" to be racist unless they have and utilize the power to oppress another ethnic member or group. But we do see this phenomenon increasing, such as when a young female employee chooses to fire an older male employee just because she wants to work with people within her age range. Or the Black supervisor who feels uncomfortable having a gay employee in the department because of the supervisor's personal beliefs and tries to get the employee transferred. This is what happens to anyone who allows personal preferences to turn into feelings of superiority and entitlement and then decides to act on them.

Show me an individual engaging in *isms* and I will show you that same individual has a lake full of insecurities, low self-worth, self-hate, and ignorance, or else has been subjected to heavy societal conditioning toward intolerance. Often times we place barriers between others and ourselves, filtering out or ignoring that which is not familiar. Many marginalized people speak of *feeling invisible,* while others, in positions of power (such as white males), feel they are held responsible for the troubles of the entire globe. These discussions take place in an organizational climate where people feel alienated from the dominant organizational culture and its position of power and privilege.

UNDERSTANDING PERCEPTION

Philosopher Georg W. F. Hegel introduced the *Standpoint Theory* early in the nineteenth century. He studied the relationship of the American slave and the "master," to try and understand the perspective of each and the influence of social hierarchies on how an individual experiences the same situation. His theory was relevant in its conclusion that *you cannot see beyond where you stand.* Many feminist researchers would later adopt the conclusions of the Standpoint Theory to advance the cause of equality between the sexes. Professor Julia T. Woods in her book, *Gendered Lives: Communication, Gender and Culture,* does an excellent job of examining this theory and its modern-day applications.

There is a delightful children's book I use in my Intercultural Communication training to teach this important theory on perspective. It is entitled *Fish Is Fish* by Leo Lionni. It is the story of a tadpole and a minnow who grew up together in a pond. They were inseparable friends. As they grew, the tadpole began to sprout legs, much to the dismay of his friend. The minnow could not understand why his friend was changing. The tadpole tried to explain he was a frog, but the minnow, now growing into a full-fledged fish, would not hear of it. One day the frog hops out of the pond to experience his world. When he returns for a visit, he explains to the fish that he has seen incredible creatures and goes on to tell the fish about birds, cows, and people. As he describes them, the fish sees each creature as a reflection of him: fish-birds, fish-cows, and fish-people. The fish was so curious about the world of his friend that he gave his tail a mighty whack and threw himself onto the bank. There he lay, gasping for air and if his frog friend had not been nearby to push him back into the pond, he would have died. Once back in the water, he had a new appreciation for his world, which he felt must be the most beautiful of all worlds (ethnocentrism). He surmised that his friend was right: fish is fish. It is a wonderful story full of many lessons about our issues of diversity. None of us can see beyond where we are unless we put on the lenses of others. We do this through respect and contact with others. Oftentimes, problems between co-cultures at work can be solved by being open to listening and communicating with the "stranger" in the next cubicle. It is our lack of global awareness that separates us.

CULTURE AND VALUES THAT IMPACT THE WORKPLACE

Our differences go far beyond the fact that people eat and dress differently. We are the person we are encultured or socialized to be. We gain our perception and *worldview* (the lens through which we evaluate the world around us) through the process of socialization. This is the process of creating a culture that is shared by the members of the society. It is during this process that we develop our values, attitudes, and beliefs. Values are at the core of a society's perspective on issues such as marriage, rearing children, capital punishment, religion, politics, women's rights, foreign policy, personal responsibility, work, and all other societal concerns of how we view the world. From these values we develop the attitudes that we turn into our beliefs. These beliefs become our societal norms. We learn our culture at an early age through the messages we receive from proverbs, fables, folktales, media, family, religion, education, and other carriers of the societal framework.

There has been a lot of examination into American values. According to Larry A. Samovar and Richard E. Porter, authors of *Communication between Cultures,* it is not easy to identify the exact values that clearly define American culture. Our history of slavery, migration, and immigration vastly differs from that of many cultures and their older, more homogeneous populations. However, the authors were able to identify key values that represent the worldview of the dominant culture of the United States (white, male, and of European descent). The seven (7) values in Figure 7.4 are: (1) individualism, (2) equality, (3) materialism, (4) science and technology, (5) progress and change, (6) work and leisure, and (7) competition (see Application 7.1). It is interesting to note that these become the fabric of how we structure our politics, religion, education, and economy.

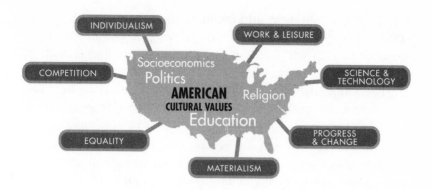

Figure 7.4 American Cultural Values

When we examine values from a more global perspective, we see the relationship we share with other cultures. Samovar explains that there are cultural patterns common to the world but they are approached differently; we term this culture-general. Take a look at *value dimensions,* as presented by Geert Hofstede in *Culture's Consequences: International Differences in Work-Related Values.* These dimensions take values that are

Application 7.1 - Values at Work

Take a moment to think about the American cultural values listed in Figure 7.4.

Do you recognize them in your life? How about your workplace? How is the job environment structured to support the value system of the organization?

Examine the following list and see if you can identify the value under which each element can be placed: promotions, appraisals, vacation, computer literacy, shareholders, employee of the month, and corporate earnings. Can you see the cause-effect relationship between cultural values and the organizational culture?

common to all cultures and examine them based on the broad spectrum with which they are infused within a culture. It will be valuable to examine three of these value dimensions and how they relate to cross-cultural communication in the workplace.

The value dimension of *individualism* versus *collectivism* was introduced in the chapter on Small-Group Communication. At issue is the value a society places on individual merit as a barometer of its stability or success. An individualistic culture sees the individual as the single most important unit of a society. A collective culture values in-group versus out-group identification, and an individual is valued only to the degree that the person is a part of the in-group. But let's focus on how the individual-collective contrast impacts cross-cultural relationships at work.

It is easy to see how an organization can comprise both individual and collective ideologies. Within U.S. institutions we strongly value individual merit, the competition that allows the "cream to rise to the top." We also understand and promote the value of teams and corporate unity. However, individual merit is the prevailing notion that drives the aspirations of most U.S. workers. Individualism is such an important value to us, we are often labeled *hyper-individualistic*. We want to be recognized for our individual contributions and awarded for our individual merit. Not all of our coworkers see it this way, and we definitely do not work in a global marketplace that is structured on the same principles. Have you ever noticed how the co-cultures in your organization tend to find one another and congregate together when the opportunity arises? You may do it yourself. Have you noticed how some coworkers are satisfied to be recognized in relation to their team or department identity? Their individual contribution is minimized under the larger significance of the collective input. What about the coworkers who cannot say enough about their personal contributions, and perhaps rightly so? If they do not, who will? Earlier, we introduced the concept of co-opetition. This is a blending of the two ideologies, recognizing our cultural values of individualism and also the importance of the collective mind-set to advance organizational goals. The next time you judge a coworker as being too competitive or lacking in ambition, remember that these are traits of conditioning and can be changed when you have the knowledge and tools.

The value dimension of *power distance* is the degree to which a culture accepts stratification of individual power and placement. High power-distance cultures are more comfortable with what could be perceived as caste-type placements, which are based on factors that change from culture to culture, such as family name, birthright and heritage, religious caste, and so on. Low power-distance cultures expect that everyone in the society should have the same opportunities as the next person; everyone should be equal. The United States, for example, places equality as one of its basic values. Think for a moment how such a value relates to global policies regarding democracy, dictatorship, free enterprise, and monopolization. The U.S. organizational framework is based on a low power-distance framework. We believe that anyone can aspire to be a corporate giant. We allow opportunities for everyone to rise within the corporate structure, at least in theory. This can often be a point of contention, for some believe the playing field is not as even as our society purports it to be. What about members of the organizational culture who come from high power-distance cultures? Might they suffer from stagnation because they believe that their "place" in the organizational culture is not for them to question? Might they also be the silent members of the organization, less likely to speak out about problems of discrimination or exploitation?

The value dimension of *uncertainty avoidance* is the proclivity of a culture to filter out that which is unfamiliar. The more homogeneous a society, the more likely it is to engage in high uncertainty avoidance, as opposed to those cultures that are more heterogeneous and more accepting of diversity. Low uncertainty-avoidance cultures tend to display tolerance for what may be considered out of the mainstream. By contrast, cultures that are high in uncertainty avoidance may find change difficult within an organization. They may not "mix" well with other members of the organization whom they find "strange." Cultures that are low in uncertainty avoidance make room for differences even when those differences make the mainstream uncomfortable. The organizational culture in the United States is based in low uncertainty avoidance and thus will make room for those who are not a part of the mainstream, dominant culture. When this is not done, voices cry out for justice and inclusion, and they usually win. Such has been the case throughout U.S. history, as witnessed by the victories of the civil rights and suffrage movements.

Once again, we can turn to the anthropoligist Edward T. Hall for an important concept. His book *Beyond Culture* describes *high-context* versus *low-context* cultures. The idea refers in part to the amount of information built into the environment. Cultures that are well established, have long histories, and are mainly homogeneous also tend to be high context—having lots of cultural information embedded into the environment. Low-context cultures tend to have a younger history and to be more heterogeneous, with fewer members of the society sharing a common history. This is a significant factor in the amount of verbal and nonverbal communication shared between individuals in a society or organization. If the messages are imbedded within the environment, there is less need for verbal explanation. Here we see why silence can be valued in some cultures and not in others, or how some rituals appear to be innate to certain groups when these rituals or traditions are a matter of intergenerational sharing. Are there members of your organizational culture who tend to value silence more than others? Speak out less? What about institutions where there has been little change over the years in philosophy and personnel? What messages appear to be a part of the "silent code" of "that's just how we do things around here"? Examine in Figure 7.5 cultures that were identified by Hall as being at one end or the other of the spectrum. What happens when high-context viewpoints

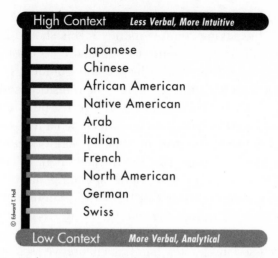

High Context   *Less Verbal, More Intuitive*

Japanese
Chinese
African American
Native American
Arab
Italian
French
North American
German
Swiss

© Edward T. Hall

Low Context   *More Verbal, Analytical*

Figure 7.5 High to Low Context Cultural Spectrum. Adapted from E. T. Hall.

meet their counterparts in the organizational culture or at the global negotiation table?

Another very interesting classification for analyzing cultural patterns examines the way that a society answers the questions of what should be valued or of what guides should be used to determine how one should live. F. R. Kluckhohn and F. L. Strodtbeck, in their *Variations in Value Orientations,* developed a list of *value orientations,* basic questions that the authors propose every society tries to answer for its members, the building blocks of a society's worldview—questions such as:

- What is the character of human nature?
- What is the relation of humankind to nature?
- What is the orientation toward time?
- What is the value placed on activity?
- What is the relationship of people to one another?

Let's examine just one of the areas and how it plays a role within our organizational functioning—a culture's orientation toward time. How do we value time in our culture? Have you ever heard the saying "time is money"? This should give you a hint. Futuristic cultures tend to value the technological advances that save time and advance the culture's global outreach. Past-oriented cultures value their history and tend to defer to it when making decisions concerning the future. Change is judged by how much it affects what the society considers to be its very important past. Present-oriented cultures value the present moment as the measurement of what is important. These cultures may value spending more time with family. An example of this can be seen in cultures that take a period of time off during the middle of the day to gather with members of their in-group; for instance, to have a siesta.

As discussed in Chapter 2, in U.S. culture we look at time as a commodity. We are what is termed *monochronic* or *M-time,* valuing time as it is segmented into activities that define our daily lives. Members of monochronic cultures live by the clock and frame their lives around activities that take place according to a prescribed schedule. *Polychronic, P-time,* cultures have a relationship with time that is seasonal and communal. They segment time according to their relationship to nature, such as harvests and the seasons, and to rituals of the community. Time is segmented according to communal responsibilities. Cultures that are individualistic tend to be monochronic, while cultures that are collective tend to be more polychronic. When these perspectives on time collide, the dominant members of the culture will determine which framework is to be adhered to. This is a very interesting phenomenon to observe in the United States, where so many migrants and immigrants come from more polychronic cultures and have to make cultural adjustments to "be on time" as they try and fit into the organizational environments where they go to work.

The above value dimensions and cultural patterns are just a few of a wide variety of culture-general variables that interculturalists have examined over the years to better understand humankind's organization of itself in relation to its world. Communication is the medium through which this is done.

NONVERBAL COMMUNICATION IS CULTURALLY BOUND

Revisit Chapter 2 on Nonverbal Communication. Consider the variables of space, time, touching, paralanguage, and other non-verbal cues that add to the varying experiences that individuals are having in the workplace, depending on each person's culture. How do these deeply ingrained nonverbal messages come together in the workplace experience of working with strangers? Think about the difficulty many people encounter when working with those whose accent is difficult for their ears to decipher. What about the coworker whose cultural understanding of hygiene is not the same as a cubicle mate's? Space and spatial relationships are set by cultural norms. As explained earlier, U.S. spatial relationships are very defined and strictly adhered to. It's a frequently reoccurring complaint in the workplace that someone's space is being invaded. This may happen between the sexes, or between members of cultures that do not have the same views of physical space. As we discussed in Chapter 3, it is very important to maintain empathy for those who just do not know the cultural mores of the dominant patterns of nonverbal communication. We need to look at and deal with others from a global lens. This is where we experience Porter and Samovar's culture-specific concept, which encourages us to learn about the unique expressions of cultures, just as we might learn languages like Japanese or Swahili. Our differences are easy to move beyond once we acknowledge the critical fact that they must and do exist AND that they invite an organizational environment of incredible innovation and global possibilities!

GLOBAL COMMUNITY

Our organizations are a reflection of the global marketplace we are all increasingly operating in. The global community is now our workplace. Humanity's history of explorers and conquistadors, imperialism and colonialism, has led us to globalism. Add a dash of industrialism, capitalism, and the futurism of technology and we have a world where *others* are hard to escape. You would think, what with global terrorism, territorial wars, ethnic cleansing, tribalism and separatism, global warming, and today's culture wars, that by now we would understand the interdependence we all have with one another. We obviously still lack the understanding of what global community means. So here we are. Our diamonds come from South African mines, our wine from France, our cars from Japan, our household products from China, and so on and so forth. In this age of trade agreements and trade wars, our major Fortune 500 companies no longer have all their investments tied to the United States. We had better start to get along. It is more than just a notion of "Well, one of my coworkers is _____." Do you know this coworker? Do you understand the unique perspective they bring to the table of innovation and decision making? (See Application 7.2.)

There has always been a survivalist way of thinking that places different people along a spectrum of comparative worth and views the resources of the planet as limited. Darwinist viewpoints abound in separatists' rhetoric even today. But the reality is that we share a common destiny as humankind. I am reminded of an advertising billboard I saw recently that displayed a Hispanic woman in front of a house. To paraphrase from memory, her message was this: "They screamed at me from their passing car, 'GO HOME!' I was standing in my own front yard." Why do individuals feel they have the right to claim what is not theirs to claim? The answer is that so many are disconnected from their own heritages. The major way this disconnection shows itself is in no longer being able to speak or connect with the language of your ethnic origin. Do you speak the language of your ancestors? Do you feel a connection with your ethnic heritage?

DIVERSITY AND THE WORKPLACE

One of the exercises I often have team members perform is to research their ancestral heritage. I get the greatest amount of re-

Application 7.2 - Real Inclusion

Take a minute to examine the makeup of your organization's decision-making bodies—board of advisers, president's cabinet, top management.

Is there truly a reflection of the members of your organization? If you are in a leadership position or have real access to someone who is, take time to ask the hard questions of your governing bodies. Do we truly value diversity of thought, innovation, problem solving, creativity?

Are the co-culture members who take part still a reflection of dominant culture attitudes? How can the organization be a true reflection of the individuals who work there and the clients we serve? Has the organization intentionally kept a sterile environment so it does not have to be inclusive?

In a short minute, we will have no choice! Which one is it, choice or force?

Co-opetition is the key!

sistance concerning this assignment from European-Americans and African-Americans, respectively. Many Euro-Americans have been taught to believe that they are American only and that they have the rights and privileges of the dominant culture afforded to them by their "founding fathers." Many no longer question where these men came from, or who was already settled on the land when the newcomers arrived. Many engage in what Mary C. Waters, in her *Ethnic Options: Choosing Identities in America,* terms *symbolic ethnicity,* which means acknowledging their cultural heritage when it suits them, such as celebrating Saint Patty's Day. By contrast, there are groups whose members have no choice but to be *ethnic* all day long. The cultural majority can experience an attitude of entitlement that in turn may breed a mentality of "us versus them," where every-one else is looked on as the *stranger*. Some participants resist the assignment but come away marveling at how much they have to be proud of in the wealth of cultural heritage they ig-nored for so long. African-American participants, and others who cannot trace their lineage, find it difficult to come face to face with their missing history. Most of the other participants have a strong connection to their ethnic and/or cultural group-ings, a connection that is easily identifiable and present in their lives. What is the purpose?

So we can all realize that we all come from somewhere, and it is the unique blend of these heritages that have made our country great. I strongly contend that it is the "let's just be human" mentality that does nothing to advance the reality of the global community. It breeds ignorance, which breeds contempt. Don't take my word for it; just turn on any international news program. The Southern Poverty Law Center reports a 300 per-cent increase in the formation of U.S.-based hate groups over the past decade. In 2006, they report, the United States had 844 hate groups. The targets of such hate groups are varied: ethnic groups, the government, women, religious ideologies that differ from the group's own, gender discrimination, and so on. There is no end to the list of what some find intolerable. Globalism is the condition that creates work environments bringing many differing people together and where there is the need for cul-tural relativism, the live-and-let-live manifesto. What happens when these differences show up in the workplace?

THE "OTHER" IN THE WORKPLACE

Ponder the cultural values and dimensions we discussed above. People are really bringing difference to the mix. Oftentimes, these differences are hard to express because it is hard to find the "appropriate language" and there is a discomfort level. Let's examine your particular experiences communicating across cultures in the workplace. Who are the individuals within your team, department, or entire organization who do not have the same accent as you or skin color or gender preference? Can you name one person? Two? Three? More than five? If you do know "others," when was the last time you engaged them in conversation that was personally validating for them? I have a very diverse mix of associates. This is not necessarily because I am drawn to every type of person, but I have made a conscious effort to broaden my circle of associates to include others who do not share my unique brand of seeing the world. I introduce them to my tastes in music, food, art, and sociopolitical viewpoints. In turn, I listen to and entertain theirs. I see this is not the experience most people are having at work. Yes, they are polite to one another and *work* together when required, but . . .

I also notice, when I visit the homes of these same individuals, that I am usually the only person outside of their cultural or ethnic circle. Most people live very homogeneous lives, even in the very heterogeneous United States. Too often, my experiences on boards, advisories, and other power-sharing groups have reeked of tokenism or else have been the exception to the rule. And then there are the times when I feel invisible to those who did not expect to see me there, or my conversation may not be inviting to them. I travel pretty widely and experience a variety of people, but I truly do not see enough examples of people trying to move beyond what is familiar. Who are you including at work?

Is your circle wider than your point of view?

You may ask, "Why should we, if we are all allowed to have our preferences?" As discussed, we can no longer afford to wear the blinders and filters of exclusivity. We must prepare ourselves to be global citizens and excel in the global marketplace. This is something that we, as an individualistic culture, have a very hard time doing. We see the world through very narrow lenses that are increasingly being recognized as counterproductive to global economic and environmental health. I am not personally advocating a change in our individualistic, democratic, capitalistic ideals; however, there are other worldviews that have paradigms of success to offer that we may well benefit from. Do they have a right to coexist? Can we? The "us versus them" rhetoric of 9/11 (on both sides) and the aftermath of war and global terrorism are clear examples of hate, fear, and intolerance along cultural and ideological lines. These are people with different worldviews, fighting one another. But they are also the same people with whom we must conquer global warming together, harvest and feed the planet together, and share fuel and water. Many will say, "But my reality tells me that I have to look out for myself at work. I have to take care of my own."

How long will YOUR own last if OUR own is brought to destruction?

We must all come to the table of sharing ideas and advances that foster health, prosperity, and peace in the global marketplace!

JILL'S DAY

Jill's reticence in the lunchroom to sit and talk with Emiko gave witness to the hundreds of individuals every day who talk themselves out of getting to know others. It's called fear. Jill sat there for almost half the lunch period contemplating if she should go talk to Emiko and what she would say. These are the types of inhibitions that keep us from experiencing life to the fullest. Go for it!

INCLUSION IN THE WORKPLACE

The world is really the imagination, hopes, fears, and dreams of our minds. We gained knowledge of this in Chapter 1. Our individual imagination, once spoken and acted on, creates the movie that we live in and invite others to share. Our world, of course, includes the block we live on, the organization we work in, the building we worship in, and all other creations of our vast intellect. Why can't we speak, act, and work in harmony? We cannot as long as we engage in the "our way or the highway" philosophy. It is mind boggling to think that with all the advancements of technology, health, and global education, with all the millions who profess to worship a higher power, we cannot live in peace. But without recognizing that our basic commonality is the power of communication and the right use of it, we will never surface from the anguish we have created right here on earth. Our organizations are only a microcosm of our communities. You must start the process in your own movie. Which takes us back where we started, step one. It is your self-love that enables you to allow others to exist in peace and the self-actualization of their own destinies. From this step you ascend to experiences that become the grand performance of your life! This is it—the movie has started!

Communication IS the Performance of Life.

BECOMING A CROSS-CULTURAL BRIDGE THROUGH CULTURAL COMPETENCY

Become a Cross-Cultural Bridge in your workplace, connecting people to one another. Share the culture-general and culture-specific knowledge you have learned in this chapter and from your further exploration. But first, start within by cleaning your lake of all the slime that perpetuates dissatisfaction with self. *Get rid of the emotional wounds* that keep you scarred and scared to reach out to others. Break the *agreements* that do not enhance a philosophy of mental and emotional health. *Exercise compassion* for yourself that you may exercise it toward others. Being less critical of yourself will help you to be less critical of others. This is especially important in the workplace where opposing ideas are always an issue to contend with. As you create this *whole person* attitude, engaging in cross-cultural communication will be much easier. You will become *more open and tolerant* to differences. You will engage in more *empathetic listening*. You will *use communication that is supportive* and *inclusive*. You will become *less tolerant of isms* within your communication climates. Your *circle of comfort will widen*. Your life *will become more interesting and adventurous*. You will join the circle of humanity. It's an incredible place to be! And that's my WORD.

Q & A Intercultural Communication

Dear PS,

Q: I have worked at my job for over 23 years. I have to admit that the organizational culture today is vastly different than just 10 years ago. I feel a bit awkward around a lot of new folks who don't look like me or seem to think the way we normally think in our department. I've got to admit I wish things were the way they used to be.

A: This is a typical response to organizational change, especially if you are a member of the dominant workplace culture. First, it is important that you are acknowledging your discomfort. The next step is to ask why. Is the company suffering because of the change in its organizational makeup? If the company is not doing as well, is it the fault of the new members or is it a sign of the economic times we are experiencing? Are you uncomfortable because of new competition? How does age play a factor? There are a lot of variables that may be playing a role in your discomfort. Many go through life never having the opportunity that you now have to expand your horizons and perspective. Think out of box before you become the box. Give the new culture a chance and see the level of adventure and creativity it adds to your life, not to mention the benefit your years of experience bring to the mix—they need you!

Q: I have received a couple of complaints that I have a tendency to invade my coworkers' space. I try to not get too close, but I guess I am just not aware. I don't get it.

A: Understand the information shared in Chapter 2 on U.S. spatial patterns. Are you from a culture that looks at personal space differently? Knowledge is the key to change. Study the NVC of the organizational culture and be patient with yourself as you make adjustments. Also, if a colleague appears offended, share that you are adjusting to the cultural differences in spatial patterns and request that the person be patient and empathetic. Your orientation program may want to incorporate NVC as a part of organizational training.

Q: One of my coworkers is not respectful of me, to put it lightly. I try not to think it's racism, but his words seem racially charged to me. I have tried to voice how uncomfortable I am, but he doesn't seem to get it. To make things worse, he is one of the supervisors.

A: This is a very serious concern, especially when it involves someone who has a position of authority within your department and is capable of creating damaging work experiences. I would suggest that you immediately ask for a joint meeting with this coworker and his supervisor, or another trusted manager, and that you ask for intervention. Document all contact and move forward to change the conditions.

Q: I have a coworker who wears her cultural costume several times a week. I find it a bit distracting, but I do not know how to share my feelings.

A: You are probably not aware that the word "costume" carries with it meanings that diminish the cultural relevance of your coworker's clothing. Your statement that she wears the clothing several times a week should be a clear indicator that this is her normal wardrobe. You will find cultural sensitivity training very valuable and enlightening. Now, this is not to say that everything worn to work is appropriate. And yes, there can be clothing considered highly distracting. If so, those responsible should handle the situation. However, this does not seem to be the case in your instance.

Q: I have a coworker who acts so afraid to stand up for herself. She has let several promotions pass her by that should have been hers. It really baffles me. She's real smart and a good worker. And she has really mastered English in her five years here.

A: This may be a situation that involves *power distance,* a concept introduced earlier in this chapter. She may come from a culture where power distance is high, so that she sees her place in life as something that doesn't change. You may want to privately discuss the situation with her to at least make sure she understands her opportunities. However, do not assume everyone is ambitious in the same way. Reread the section.

New Beginnings

"In the beginning was the Word. . . ."
—The King James Bible, John 1:1

Jill Smith was a longtime colleague of mine with a history very familiar to me. We have spent many hours working through the destructive communication patterns she had turned into habits over the years. She is on the road to personal recovery. A couple of years ago she left the job described in her story, and her cast members have changed. She is writing a new script now, with coworkers she respects, and has an attitude of collective productivity. Through persistence and application of learned strategies and principles, we have broken through the enemy's stronghold and figured out its primary weakness: our ability to use thoughts and words as our tool of victory. No longer can the tactics of self-doubt, victimization, and self-centeredness be the primary ingredients of our daily interactions in the workplace. We understand the primary objective: to use the power of thoughts and words to create a workplace communication climate that is supportive, productive, and nurturing for ourselves and others. We have armed ourselves with knowledge. This knowledge plus action equals power! You are now equipped with the tools of victory. You are gaining control of your Intrapersonal Communication by understanding how it sets the foundation for all other communication experiences, including how your life movie plays out. You know that your Interpersonal Communication is a direct reflection of yourself through the mirror messages you receive from others. You recognize that making room for another's reality is the primary function of interpersonal relationships in the workplace. You have harnessed your Nonverbal Communication skills so that there is congruency between what you say and how you say it. Your Small-Group Communication experiences are now filled with personal integrity, communication ease, and the collective energy of bringing your individual best to the whole. Public Communication is no longer a nightmare but a satisfying expression of your skills and abilities for all to see and hear. Mass Communication is a tool that you have learned to rightly perceive and apply to aspects of your work life that lead to enrichment and purposeful awareness. And finally, you have joined the ranks of the Intercultural Communication elite by becoming a Cultural Bridge bringing people together in the spirit of diversity and inclusion. Communication is the science of human existence. Learn the formulas that make your movie worth starring in. It all begins and ends with the words that not only create your reality but are the connecting web of the human experience.

Watch your thoughts, they become
Your words.

Watch your words, they become
Your actions.

Watch your actions, they become
Your habits.

Watch your habits, they become
Your character.

Watch your character, for it becomes
Your destiny.

—Adapted from Frank Outlaw

We have defeated the enemy and every day we add new victors to our ranks, erasing centuries of self-defeat. After reading this, we hope you will join us by applying the Communication Staircase Model we have shared and empower yourself with the greatest gift you have—your word. Have I conquered all the skills I have shared with you? Am I starring in my own movie? Not totally, but I'm working on the Art *and* Science of Communication, EVERY DAY!

Have a wonderful day. It's always your choice!
HCI, LLC/NJM

Index

Index

187

INDEX

Index

189

INDEX

190

Index

INDEX

Index

Mistakes, public communication and, 115
Misunderstanding, in dyadic communication, 68–69
Money, time as, 168
Monitoring. *See* Self-monitoring
Monochronic cultures, 42, 43, 168
Moore, Michael, 47
Morale, fixing sagging, 108
Motivation, 149, 151–152
  in public communication, 116–117
  via mass communication, 143, 144
Mould theory, 7
Movie creation, communication as, xxii
Movies, 61. *See also* "Life movie" analogy
M-time cultures, 168
Multicultural audiences, in public communication, 117, 121
Multiple perspectives/viewpoints:
  in group projects, 92
  in small-group communication, 97
Musical composer, of "life movie," 62
Myopia, of listeners, 128–129

Native Americans, intercultural communication and, 157
Nature, culture and, 167–168
Negative colleagues, 26, 88–89
Negative thoughts, 25–26
  self-monitoring of, 15–16, 18
Negativity, in dyadic communication, 74–75
Nervousness:
  impromptu speaking and, 132
  in public communication, 117
Networks:
  in dyadic communication, 69
  formal and informal communication, 102–104
Neutral-detached conflict resolution, 75–76
Noise, 80
  in dyadic communication, 67, 70–71
  in group communication, 105
  in small-group communication, 98
Nonlistening behaviors, 81, 82
Nonverbal codes, 30
Nonverbal communication (NVC), xviii, xix, xx, 25, 29–54, 182
  body movements as, 40–42
  defined, 29–30
  in intercultural communication, 169
  paralanguage as, 37–40
  professional appearance as, 32–37
  professional voice as, 37–40
  public communication and, 116–117, 118, 123–124, 124–125
  seven functions of, 29–32, 33
  smell as, 50–52
  space and distance in, 45–48, 49

time and timing in, 42–45
touching behavior as, 48–50
Nonverbal messages, in dyadic communication, 68–69
Nonverbal responses, in dyadic communication, 72
Noorda, Raymond John "Ray," 95
Notes of a Native Son (Baldwin), 155

Office chatter, in organizations, 103, 104
Office space, 47. *See also* Organizational space
Olfactory communication, 32, 33, 50–52
Openness:
  in impromptu speaking, 129–130
  intercultural communication and, 176
Opinion leaders, in mass communication, 136–137
Organizational communication. *See* Small-group/organizational communication
Organizational space, 48, 49. *See also* Office space
Organizations. *See also* Small-group/organizational communication
  conflict resolution in, 102
  ethnic makeup of, 171
  formal and informal communication networks in, 102–104
  impromptu speaking in, 129–131
  individualism versus collectivism in, 164–165
  intercultural communication and, 157–158, 175, 176–177
  leadership in, 99
  mass communication and, 141, 142–143
  persuasion in, 146–147, 148, 151–163
  prejudice and, 160
  touching behavior in, 49, 50
"Other," the, in workplace, 172–174
Other people's stuff, 150
Out-groups, 93–94

Pac-Man game analogy, 57, 76
Paralanguage:
  as nonverbal communication, 31, 32, 33, 37–40
  in public communication, 116, 121, 123–124
  leadership and, 100
Participation, in dyadic communication, 69
Passion, in leadership communication, 101
Pass It On, xiii
Passive-aggressive conflict resolution, 75–76
Past, 42
Past-oriented cultures, 168
Pathos, persuasion via, 147
Patriarchal system, mass communication in, 135–136
Paying attention, in listening, 80

193

INDEX

Index

Index

INDEX